LIVING A BIBLICAL FAITH

LIBRARY OF LIVING FAITH

JOHN M. MULDER, General Editor

LIVING

A

BIBLICAL FAITH

BY

DONALD H. JUEL

THE WESTMINSTER PRESS
PHILADELPHIA

BOOK DESIGN BY DOROTHY ALDEN SMITH

First edition

Published by The Westminster Press ®
Philadelphia, Pennsylvania

PRINTED IN THE UNITED STATES OF AMERICA
9 8 7 6 5 4 3 2 1

Library of Congress Cataloging in Publication Data

Juel, Donald.
   Living a biblical faith.

   (Library of living faith)
   Bibliography: p.
   1. Christian life—Lutheran authors. I. Title.
II. Series.
BV4501.2.J83   1982   248.4'841   82-8652
ISBN 0-664-24429-7 (pbk.)   AACR2

For Lynda

CONTENTS

FOREWORD

The word "theology" comes from two Greek words—
theos ("God") and *logos* ("word" or "thought"). Theology
is simply words about God or thinking about God. But for
many Christians, theology is remote, abstract, baffling,
confusing, and boring. They turn it over to the professionals—the theologians—who can ponder and inquire into
the ways of God with the world.

This series, Library of Living Faith, is for those Christians who thought theology wasn't for them. It is a collection of ten books on crucial doctrines or issues in the Christian faith today. Each book attempts to show why our
theology—our thoughts about God—matters in what we
do and say as Christians. The series is an invitation to
readers to become theologians themselves—to reflect on
the Bible and on the history of the church and to find their
own ways of understanding the grace of God in Jesus
Christ.

The Library of Living Faith is in the tradition of another
series published by Westminster Press in the 1950s, the
Layman's Theological Library. This new collection of
volumes tries to serve the church in the challenges of the
closing decades of this century.

The ten books are based on the affirmation of the Letter
to the Ephesians (4:4–6): "There is one body and one

9

Spirit, just as you were called to the one hope that belongs
to your call, one Lord, one faith, one baptism, one God and
Father of us all, who is above all and through all and in all."
Each book addresses a particular theme as part of the
Christian faith as a whole; each book speaks to the church
as a whole. Theology is too important to be left only to the
theologians; it is the work and witness of the entire people
of God.

But, as Ephesians says, "grace was given to each of us
according to the measure of Christ's gift" (Eph. 4:7), and
the Library of Living Faith tries to demonstrate the diversity of theology in the church today. Differences, of course,
are not unique to American Christianity. One only needs
to look at the New Testament and the early church to see
how "the measure of Christ's gift" produced disagreement
and conflict as well as a rich variety of understandings of
Christian faith and discipleship. In the midst of the unity
of the faith, there has never been uniformity. The authors
in this series have their own points of view, and readers
may argue along the way with the authors' interpreta-
tions. But each book presents varying points of view and
shows what difference it makes to take a particular theological position. Sparks may fly, but the result, we hope,
will be a renewed vision of what it means to be a Christian
exhibiting in the world today a living faith.

These books are also intended to be a library—a set of
books that should be read together. Of course, not everything is included. As the Gospel of John puts it, "There are
also many other things which Jesus did; were every one of
them to be written I suppose that the world itself could not
contain the books that would be written" (John 21:25).
Readers should not be content to read just the volume on
Jesus Christ or on God or on the Holy Spirit and leave out
those on the church or on the Christian life or on Christianity's relationship with other faiths. For we are called to
one faith with many parts.

The volumes are also designed to be read by groups of people. Writing may be a lonely task, but the literature of the church was never intended for individuals alone. It is for the entire body of Christ. Through discussion and even debate, the outlines of a living faith can emerge.

For centuries, Christians have agonized over the question of what it meant to be a Christian. Using the letter to the Ephesians to organize his approach to this age-old issue, Donald H. Juel analyzes how the new life in Christ was seen in the New Testament and how it might be viewed today. He describes tension—between the old world and the new, between justification by faith alone and the structure of life in grace. "That tension needs to be preserved," he writes. "Christians cannot abandon the old world in favor of another, since this is the only world there is. Nor can we settle with things as they are. The gospel is still a surprise, a shock, a message that demands new skins for new wine." Dr. Juel teaches New Testament literature at Luther-Northwestern Theological Seminary, and he has previously taught at Indiana University and Princeton Theological Seminary. He is an ordained Lutheran minister and has written *Messiah and Temple* (1977), *An Introduction to New Testament Literature* (1978), and *Proclamation: Pentecost* (1980).

JOHN M. MULDER
Louisville Presbyterian Theological Seminary
Louisville, Kentucky

INTRODUCTION

> For once you were darkness, but now you are light in the
> Lord; walk as children of light. (Eph. 5:8)

In its infancy, the Christian movement offered real alternatives. Believers could understand the difference between "once" and "now." Confessing Jesus entailed clear-cut decisions. For some it meant abandoning the worship of idols; for others it meant living with people formerly separated by custom or religious heritage; for many it meant breaking family ties, often accepting expulsion from social groups. Commitment to Jesus involved sacrifices, but it also offered genuine alternatives.

As Western Christians we have more difficulty viewing Christianity as a distinctive way of life. Many in our society regard themselves as Christians, yet it is difficult to identify features that set them apart from others. It would be hard to prove that Christians are habitually more loving than others. Apart from a few striking exceptions, believers in Jesus have not distinguished themselves as civil rights leaders. Mainline churches have seldom served as advocates for the poor and dispossessed. Christian marriages end in divorce in approximately the same proportion as non-Christian marriages. Though almost half the Christians in the United States describe themselves as "born again," the life of faith in general lacks real drama. In most communities Christians behave much like their neighbors and may even be indistinguishable from them apart from Sunday schedules.

To compound the problem, there is a steady stream of books and pamphlets arguing for "Christian" positions that seem almost diametrically opposed. On one side are Christian rightists, pictured on television specials with automatic weapons, preparing for the coming battle with "Jews, blacks, and Hispanics" in which believers will be obliged to defend Jesus with force. On the opposing side are Christian leftists, pronouncing the blessings of the church on guerrilla movements intent upon overthrowing fascist governments in Latin America. Church officials in South Africa defend apartheid, while Christian leaders elsewhere in the world demand that all investments in South Africa be withdrawn and that connections with churches which support apartheid be severed. Believers unable to agree about creationism or censorship end up taking their respective cases to court, providing an ironic parallel to the situation that Paul describes in his first letter to the Corinthian church (I Cor. 6:1–11).

Ours is not an age of conversation but of pronouncement. The point is eloquently made in a series of lectures, collected under the imposing title *Modern Dogma and the Rhetoric of Assent,* delivered at Notre Dame University by Wayne Booth, a teacher of English and rhetoric at the University of Chicago. Reflecting on the scene at the university during the late '60s, when confrontations were matched in intensity only by rhetoric that heralded the impossibility of reasoning with "the other side," Booth describes a view that has become dogma to modern people. Booth argues that in matters of value, rational arguments have no real force. Persuasion has to do only with passion, hype, or brute force. If civilization is to flourish, Booth argues, we must expose this false dogma and learn how to converse reasonably about things that matter, how to offer good reasons for what we believe.

His diagnosis and his prescription fit the situation within the religious community. We are divided and confused about what it means to live as Christians. But the mere imposition of authority will not solve the problem. When the Roman Catholic Church hardened its opposition to contraception, survey after survey documented increasing indifference to official policy by Catholic women, who in larger and larger numbers use contraceptives. The situation is similar in the Protestant churches when church members frequently pay little attention to the denominational pronouncements of their own church. However, erosion of respect for institutions and authorities is not good news; it leads into deeper uncertainty, doubt, and cynicism. People who feel keenly the pain of the world and think critically about the role of Christians in contemporary society will not be helped by simplistic ecclesiastical pronouncements from officials out of touch with the world. Nor will they be aided by increased passion on the part of advocates for various programs. Booth is correct: we need good reasons for believing that one view is more helpful or more appropriate than another. We must learn to think together about the faith and its implications, to understand our own views, to evaluate the arguments of those who seek to move us one way or another, and to find some common ground on which to discuss the life of faith.

The focus of our disagreements as Christians is not so much the question, What must I do to be saved? as What ought I do as one of the saved? Few within Christendom would argue that we are saved by grace or that God forgives sins or that faith in God promises eternal life. We disagree about implications. What role should the church play in society or in the political arena? Can a Christian be a homosexual? What should believers think about the women's movement? Is there specific Christian morality?

Are some occupations more "Christian" than others? Such
are the questions that divide us. Disagreement is often so
heated that families and friends agree not to talk about
religion, and we are left to talk with those with whom we
agree.

The injunction to "walk as children of light" implies that
there are some standards by which to evaluate our sundry
opinions. Historically, Christians have looked to the Bible
for such standards. The term used for the Sacred Scriptures, "canon," means standard or guideline. Most Christians, whether simple or sophisticated, literalists or practitioners of higher criticism, accord a certain priority to the
Bible in matters of faith and life. If we are to establish a
basis for conversation about the life of faith, the Scriptures
will have to be part of the common ground. But how are
the Scriptures to serve as a "canon" or standard? Few of
us would subscribe to the old practice of asking a question,
then letting the Bible fall open to a particular verse.
"Searching the Scriptures" requires effort, for the Bible
does not always speak to particular matters, and when it
does, there are sometimes conflicting opinions. We will
also have to agree on certain ground rules, since we know
that "the devil can cite Scripture for his purpose." Despite
the difficulty of such introductory matters, the Bible offers
the promise of conversation with one another.

Questions about discipleship were uppermost in the
minds of the biblical authors. Not one of the books in the
New Testament, for example, was written to convert people. Authors wrote for believers, to help them understand
what it meant to be saved, forgiven, reconciled, freed, and
baptized.

The apostle Paul wrote letters to churches that he himself had founded (with the exception of his letter to the
church at Rome). Letters served as a substitute for his
presence when he was unable to visit in person. His letters
were pastoral, serving to encourage, to combat false teach-

ing, and to give advice. Each letter had particular goals bound up with the concrete circumstances in the various churches. But all the letters are about discipleship. Paul sought to help his churches understand what it meant to live as people for whom Christ had died. His advice extended to quite ordinary matters—what kind of meat to buy at the market, whether or not to marry, what roles were appropriate to men and women in the church.

The Gospels, as stories about Jesus, are less obviously concerned with the life of faith. But the more closely we read them, the more we sense the questions lurking beneath the surface. Narratives deal with larger dimensions of life that are no less practical than the particulars in Paul's letters. Who are we? the Gospels ask. What does Jesus' ministry tell us about the world in which we live, about our prospects and our responsibilities, about our cultural and religious heritage?

The Gospels, the Epistles, even the Revelation of John were addressed to believers to help them understand what it meant to live as redeemed children of God in a world that was as yet unredeemed. Even a cursory examination of the range and variety of material in the New Testament tells us some important things about discipleship. For one thing, the life of faith cannot be understood in terms of a general principle like "love" or "servanthood." Discipleship was too closely tied to the object of faith, the crucified and risen Lord, to be reduced to abstract principles. Another observation is that discipleship was always understood concretely. Paul wrote to people, not in general, but in particular. The churches to whom he sent his letters included people named Philemon and Stephanus, Fortunatus and Euodia and Syntyche. The names are strange, reminding us that the world is larger than our own experience of it. People differed, then as now. In Galatia believers were cautious, interested in hedging their freedom in Christ with calendars and circumcision.

"For freedom Christ has set us free," Paul reminded them. The Corinthians, on the other hand, understood well the liberating power of the gospel. They had to be reminded that there are limitations even for Christians who have been set free from bondage to the law. "All things are lawful for me," Paul could argue, "but not all things are helpful." Understanding discipleship in Galatia and Corinth meant attending to the differences between the two groups of people.

Diversity within the Scriptures has always been a problem for Christians. It is no less a problem today as pluralism inside and outside the church threatens to undermine any sense of order and coherence and to destroy any basis for meaningful conversation and consensus. The early Christian movement has much to teach us about pluralism as well. The formation of a canon, a collection of books intended to serve as a measure for the life and faith of believers, was a response to pluralism and confusion that threatened to destroy the Christian movement. Selection of precisely these writings (the exact number was debated well into the Middle Ages) meant rejecting others considered inappropriate, even dangerous, for public reading in the church. In contrasting New Testament works with noncanonical literature, we can appreciate the sense in which the collection presents a unified perspective.

But unity is not the same as uniformity. New Testament authors did not produce systematic treatises on ethics. Those who seek to find in the Scriptures *the* structure of the Christian life will be disappointed—or they will be forced to impose on the Bible a uniformity that does not exist. New Testament authors wrote letters and stories. They did not impose on life an artificial regularity. They wrote for people who experienced life differently, who had a distinct angle on the world. For each group, discipleship had a special flavor and a unique shape. Interpretation that respects the richness and diversity of the Scriptures cannot reduce discipleship to a set of principles. Christians resisted creating a new law that offered answers to every question. Neither a Stoic natural law nor the unaltered Torah of Judaism would provide the needed guidelines for the life of faith. The cross of Christ which made all things new had revolutionary implications for life in the world as well as for life in the church.

Study of the Bible will not settle our disputes. It may even give rise to new ones. But it can offer us a glimpse of a world we seldom see clearly—a world at first strange, but on further reflection not very different from our own. In the struggles of Paul and Matthew and John to understand their world in the light of the gospel, and their place in it, we may see a reflection of ourselves and our struggles and possibilities. We will not react in one way; indeed, we should not. But we may find it easier to discuss with one another the highs and the lows of life in faith as we have experienced it.

Hundreds of scholars have written thousands of books about discipleship, ethics, and the dynamics of faith. I offer this modest contribution to the literature from my own perspective as a student of the New Testament and as a Lutheran, and readers may quickly recognize these influences. As I write, I have in mind all those I have known in classes and congregations and our neighborhoods who struggle to understand Christ's call to follow, people who have experienced the graciousness of God but who wish at least a glimpse of the possibilities of faithful response to the gospel. If some of them find the chapters useful, the book has served its purpose.

1

THE NEW COMMUNITY IN CHRIST

I therefore, a prisoner for the Lord, beg you to lead a life worthy of the calling to which you have been called, with all lowliness and meekness, with patience, forbearing one another in love, eager to maintain the unity of the Spirit in the bond of peace. There is one body and one Spirit, just as you were called to the one hope that belongs to your call. (Eph. 4:1–4)

Thus begins the section on ethical instruction in the letter to the Ephesians. The injunction is a convenient place to begin reflecting on the nature of the Christian life. Typical of the New Testament as a whole, this discussion of discipleship begins with a "therefore." The life of the Christian is a response. In the language of Ephesians, it is a response to a "call." The priority of God's summons is a familiar theme in the Bible. The drama of God's involvement with Israel opens with the call of Abraham in Genesis 12 and with a promise: "By you all the families of the earth shall bless themselves" (Gen. 12:3). Christians believed that God had fulfilled that promise in Jesus. He had sent his own Son for the salvation of the world. As he had once called Abraham to follow, so now he summoned all people to be disciples of Jesus the Christ.

"Therefore" has another sense. If discipleship is a response, it should be an appropriate response. There is a

21

connection between the message of salvation and the
shape of the life to which believers are called. The gospel
determines how we view discipleship. Though Christian
traditions differ in emphases, all acknowledge that the
gospel is more than an announcement that God is gracious
and loving. Other religions view God as gracious. Christians have often caricatured Judaism as a religion that
offers salvation only to those who earn it. Jews have always
known, however, that God's choice is unmerited, that God
is "merciful and gracious, slow to anger, and abounding in
steadfast love" (Ex. 34:6). What distinguished Jesus' followers from their Jewish and Gentile neighbors was not that
they viewed God as gracious. Rather, it was their insis-
tence that the nature of God's grace and the shape of a
faithful life could be understood only in the light of Jesus.
Their "good news" was news about Jesus and the God who
had raised him from the dead. Christian discipleship
means being conformed to the Christ.

Even during his ministry Jesus' disciples recognized that
following him involved new ways of living in the world,
ways many found troubling. Jesus' contemporaries saw
him as a religious man, rooted in Israel's heritage. Yet he
refused to abide by the religious traditions that offered
meaning and security to his contemporaries. He as-
sociated with the irreligious: "Now the tax collectors and
sinners were all drawing near to hear him. And the Pharisees and the scribes murmured, saying, 'This man receives
sinners and eats with them' " (Luke 15:1–2).

Pharisees were not legalists, preoccupied with their
own status, as they have often been portrayed. They were
the pietists of Jewish society, concerned to preserve their
heritage during a time of far-reaching social change and
religious decay. They resisted restricting religion to the
sacred, believing that God's law was intended for every
aspect of human life. By their public adherence to the
Torah, they also sought to provide testimony to the God

who had given the law to Moses.

Jesus' behavior puzzled such Jews. By associating with the unrighteous, even eating with them, Jesus appeared to sanction their way of life. By touching the unclean—lepers, a woman with a hemorrhage, even the dead—he risked ritual defilement. He insisted, however, that such violations of tradition were necessary in order to bring the strays back into the fold and to heal the diseased. "Those who are well have no need of a physician," he told his critics, "but those who are sick" (Mark 2:17).

Christian practice was more than an imitation of Jesus, however. The shape of their corporate lives depended not only on stories Jesus told, like the story of the prodigal son or the lost coin or the lost sheep, nor solely on his practice of including outcasts at meals. Their lives reflected events that dwarfed all others by comparison: "For I delivered to you as of first importance what I also received, that Christ died for our sins in accordance with the scriptures, that he was buried, that he was raised on the third day in accordance with the scriptures, that he appeared . . ." (I Cor. 15:3–5).

Jesus' death and resurrection placed his ministry in a new category. For his followers, the resurrection marked a new beginning for Jesus, for them, and for the whole of human history. The extraordinary event could not be contained within traditional Jewish forms of life and worship. "Christ is the end of the law," said Paul (Rom. 10:4). "New skins for new wine," said Jesus (Mark 2:22).

The importance of this gospel of Jesus' death and resurrection for understanding discipleship is evident in New Testament baptismal formulations. Only language about death and rebirth could capture the change that occurred in the lives of converts: "And you were buried with him in baptism, in which you were also raised with him through faith in the working of God who raised him from the dead. And you, who were dead in trespasses, . . . God made alive together with him, having forgiven us all our trespasses" (Col. 2:12, 13).

Baptism was understood as "incorporation into Christ," a way of becoming one with the crucified and risen Lord. The benefits of Jesus' atoning death and resurrection became theirs. The identity with Christ was expressed simply; the word "with" was added to verbs that were used of Jesus in creeds such as I Cor. 15:3–7 ("died," "buried," "raised"). When applied to believers, the language is remarkably unrestrained. You have died, Paul says to the Colossians, and you have been raised. He says the same thing using other words: "Therefore, if any one is in Christ, he is a new creation; the old has passed away, behold, the new has come" (II Cor. 5:17).

The imagery had power because baptism was not only incorporation into Christ, the initiation of a relationship with the risen Lord, but incorporation into the body of Christ—the church. The community of the baptized was the place where the new life actually took shape. Baptismal images spoke about realities that took concrete form in the life of a group. "Newness" was not an abstract idea; it referred to a way of life embodied in relationships among the faithful.

The motif that dominates discussion of the life of faith in Ephesians is unity. There is "one body," "one Spirit," "one hope," "one Lord," "one faith," "one baptism," "one God and Father of us all" (Eph. 4:4–6). Walking "worthy of your calling" means maintaining "the unity of the Spirit in the bond of peace." The letter is quite specific about the possibilities that exist for unity: Jew and Gentile can now live together. The law of Moses, whose purpose was to separate Jews from non-Jews, no longer served that function. The "dividing wall of hostility"—a reference to the barrier in the Jerusalem Temple that prevented Gentiles from entering the inner precincts—has been symbolically broken down (Eph. 2:11–22). For the author of Ephesians, the most remarkable expression of the changed situation of those "in Christ" is that "Gentiles are fellow heirs, members of the same body, and partakers of the promise in Christ Jesus through the gospel" (Eph. 3:6). Within the church, people ate together who could not even associate elsewhere.

The preoccupation with unity suggests that it was not a natural condition of society in the ancient world any more than it is in our own day. Though we experience the same sense of alienation from one another in our society, we have more difficulty sensing the potential of the gospel for reconciliation. One reason is that our view of life tends to be individualistic. We speak of ourselves more as single persons than as groups. Our American religious heritage tends to speak of sin as a personal matter that involves our individual relationship with God. Biblical authors recognized that sin also affects the way people relate to one another. The result of the Fall in Genesis is not simply that relationships with God are strained and that Adam and Eve are expelled from the garden. Society is poisoned. Cain kills his brother (Gen. 4:1–14); people brutalize one another (Gen. 4:23–24); and the world is divided into groups unable even to understand one another (Gen. 11: 1–9). God's call of Abraham is a response to a world splintered into a thousand fragments, a world at war with itself.

Churches of the Reformation have done a good job of relating the liberating power of the gospel to individual bondage. The message of justification, the declaration of forgiveness, the announcement that God accepts even the unacceptable have proved effective ways of communicating God's grace. In the last decades, we have become acutely aware of other forms of bondage—bondage to cultural patterns that foster alienation and discrimination. The civil rights movement called attention to the inequities among blacks and whites, rich and poor. The movement for women's liberation called attention to outright discrimination against women built into social patterns and into the law. The liberation movement in theology has given voice to protests from the poor and the dispossessed to whom the church, as well as the state, has given little heed. While individual Christian leaders have been at the forefront of such movements for liberation and reconciliation, churches have been less successful in relating the gospel to social and political alienation and bondage.

Diversity is a natural feature of the created order. There is nothing strange about racial differences or about the division of the race into male and female. In a world infected by sin, racial and sexual differences signify more than variety. They become occasions for separation and for discrimination. In her massive novel *The Women's Room,* Marilyn French portrays a society that makes equitable relationships between men and women impossible. Society's natural assumption that a husband's career will take precedence over his wife's, the leers of police taking testimony from a raped woman—the unfairness is overwhelming. Story after story in the book chips away at any hope of changing such deep-seated patterns of relationship between men and women. There is an almost fatalistic sense that maleness and femaleness, like other differences among humans, provide insuperable barriers to harmonious life together. We live in our own communities, with our own kind, and we seem bound in the world of our imagination to view differences as threatening, as barriers.

In the New Testament, the news of Jesus' death and resurrection spoke directly to such bondage. Consider the baptismal formula in Paul's letter to the churches of Galatia: "For as many of you as were baptized into Christ Jesus have put on Christ. There is neither Jew nor Greek, there is neither slave nor free, there is neither male nor female; for you are all one in Christ Jesus" (Gal. 3:27–28).

The words from the baptismal rite offer a very different picture of community. Baptism offers liberation from the power of sin understood as the power of alienation. "Putting on Christ" involves breaking down the barriers that divide the human family. The specific distinctions are carefully chosen. Even in the time of Plato, race, gender, and social status were the categories by which human society was defined. The same categories served as means of evaluation. One could be truly happy, Plato insisted, only as a male, a freedman, and a Greek.

The same distinctions were preserved in Jewish tradition, expressed most graphically in the prayer every Jew was obliged to pray daily:

> Blessed art Thou, O Lord our God, King of the Universe, who hast not made me a heathen.
> Blessed art Thou, O Lord our God, King of the Universe, who hast not made me a bondman.
> Blessed art Thou, O Lord our God, King of the Universe, who hast not made me a woman.
>   *(Authorized Daily Prayer Book)*

In its liturgical setting the prayer is not an expression of arrogance. It offers thanks to God for the privilege of keeping the Commandments, whose obligations fall most heavily on free Jewish males. Nevertheless, in the prayer, as in the whole Greco-Roman world, division into sexes, races, and social classes served as a means of evaluation. It is better to be male than female, better to be a Greek or a Jew than a barbarian or a Gentile, better to be upper class than lower.

Incorporation into Christ through baptism offered radically new social possibilities. The Christian community saw itself as an alternative to a world divided into unequal factions, a world bound by destructive conventions. Paul, the exclusivist Jew who after his conversion became an apostle to non-Jews, viewed the gospel as God's response to the effects of the Tower of Babel. The good news, Paul insisted, is that we can be one family again, reconciled to God and to one another: "All this is from God, who through Christ reconciled us to himself and gave us the ministry of reconciliation; that is, in Christ God was reconciling the world to himself, not counting their trespasses against them, and entrusting to us the message of reconciliation" (II Cor. 5:18–19).

The church's call to embody that ministry of liberation and reconciliation raises several practical questions. What does it mean concretely to speak of a new unity in Christ? There are still significant differences between male and female, black and white, rich and poor. In what sense are those differences no longer important? What kinds of traditions and conventions will be appropriate for a group that no longer respects the corrupt conventions of secular society? What will it mean to live out a new life-style in a world that still discriminates and evaluates in terms of gender, race, and social status? Such questions that were posed in the first churches are pertinent in our setting as well.

I propose to deal with these questions by examining one of the problems Paul discusses in his first letter to the church at Corinth. I do so for a number of reasons. The letter introduces us to a lively congregation whose problems are not very different from our own. Paul had succeeded in establishing a vital community of believers in the coastal town. He wrote, not to settle problems of heresy, but to answer practical questions the church had asked in a letter (I Cor. 7:1). Paul's advice offers a glimpse of church life, an example of his thoughts about discipleship, and some sense of the dynamics of the life of faith within the church. Knowing something about I Corinthians may also provide a basis for conversation among Christians about the nature of discipleship in contemporary society.

THE ROLE OF WOMEN IN THE CHURCH AT CORINTH

Paul sent his letter to the congregation in response to their letter in which they had posed several questions (I Cor. 7:1; 8:1; 12:1; 16:1). The questions are practical. Should we marry or not? What about marriages to unbelievers? Can we eat meat offered to idols? What are we to think about spiritual gifts? The questions are also, upon closer inspection, controversial. As Paul discovered from an unofficial delegation from the congregation, "Chloe's people," the church was in an uproar, split into factions, fighting about everything (I Cor. 1:10–12). Galatian Christians were cautious, nervous about the new possibilities the gospel set before them. The Corinthians were not at all hesitant about freedom. "All things are lawful for me" was a slogan—and Paul does not dispute its appropriateness, though he does ask if that is all there is to say (I Cor. 10:23 to 11:1). Freedom was destroying the community. Those with robust consciences ate meat offered to idols, a practice that scandalized those with more sensitive consciences. Those with more spectacular charismatic gifts flaunted them at worship, to the dismay of those who could boast no such gifts. The wealthy showed little concern for those who had little, even at the common meal. Paul's letter is an attempt to help his charges in Corinth learn how to live together without quenching the Spirit or stifling their willingness to experiment with new forms of corporate life.

The problem we will examine had to do with the role of women in the congregation. The short section (I Cor. 11: 2-16) opens with praise for the congregation: "I commend you because you remember me in everything and maintain the traditions even as I have delivered them to you" (v. 2).

The section is balanced by vs. 17–34, which begins, "But

in the following instructions I do not commend you." The matters discussed in vs. 17–34 merit Paul's censure; those in vs. 2–16 do not. The "problem" involving women does not seem to be a serious one, at least not in Paul's estimation.

The difficulty involved violation of social norms at worship. Women were apparently removing head coverings (vs. 10–13). Their behavior had become an issue. The matter may seem trivial, but the potency of dress as a social symbol is well known to anyone who remembers the anger generated by fashions and hairstyles among young people in the late '60s. Clothing symbolizes a view of the world. In first-century Greece, as in modern society, head coverings and length of hair made statements about the social order. In v. 10, Paul uses the word "authority" for women's head coverings ("That is why a woman ought to have a veil [literally, "authority"] on her head"), meaning that the veil implied acknowledgment by the women of an authority over them; veils, in other words, implied that women were subordinate. That is certainly the case today in the Near East. In his attempt to westernize Islamic society, the Shah of Iran introduced Western dress, removing veils and head coverings for women. When the Islamic revolution began, Western clothing for women provided a convenient focus for attack. Reintroduction of coverings for women symbolized a whole view of the world which the revolution sought to impose once again on Iranian society.

Removal of head coverings in Corinth symbolized a small-scale social revolution, at least within the congregation. Some sought to break with society's distinction between men and women by altering their attire. From all we know of Greco-Roman society, there is little reason to believe motivation for such a revolution came from society at large or from another religious group. Women had few rights, and even the handful of philosophers who supported some form of equality in theory did not practice social equality between male and female. We need hardly look beyond Paul's own theology for the cause of the "liberation movement" in the Corinthian church. The baptismal formula that Paul states in Gal. 3:28 reads: "There is neither Jew nor Greek, there is neither slave nor free, there is neither male nor female; for you are all one in Christ Jesus." Interestingly he mentions only Jews and Greeks, slaves and free in the Corinthian letter; "male and female" are absent (I Cor. 12:13), perhaps omitted intentionally. It seems likely that some women in the church at Corinth took seriously what had occurred in baptism. They had put on Christ. The old self they sought to remove included status under the law. Removing head coverings as an indication of their new status in Christ probably seemed an appropriate expression of their faith.

The propriety of such a revolution would seem obvious. Though Paul himself displayed little interest in "slave and free" and "male and female," he certainly believed that eliminating distinctions between Jew and Greek was an essential feature of the new faith. He insisted, furthermore, that the "spiritual truth" had to be translated into social practice. His dispute with Peter in Antioch (Gal. 2) and his angry words to the Galatians constituted an eloquent defense of social liberation.

Even if Paul did not argue for freeing slaves and liberating women, he seems to have been far more open in practice to new social patterns than most. He includes the names of women as leaders in local congregations. When he refers to his associates, Prisca and Aquila, he never refers to Prisca as "the wife of Aquila." Though Paul never advocated freeing slaves as a social program, when confronted with Onesimus, a runaway slave, he sent a letter to his friend Philemon requesting that he accept Onesimus back without penalty and that he set him free.

In the light of Paul's theological convictions and prac-

tice, his response to the situation at Corinth is somewhat
surprising. In a few verses he dispenses with the matter of
head coverings. In the preceding discussion of food offered to idols (I Cor. 8–10), Paul faces a similar problem.
"Strong" Christians with robust consciences had no difficulty eating what had been offered to idols, knowing that
idols have no real existence, but weaker believers were
scandalized by any association with idolatry. Paul's discussion of the matter requires three chapters and he never
does take sides. In ch. 11, on the other hand, he seems to
side unambiguously with those in the church who find
social liberation of women offensive and disruptive. He
advises women to put on their head coverings. When
faced with the possibility of supporting even a small-scale
social revolution, breaking down distinctions between
male and female, Paul backed off. Paul's investment in this
issue was obviously far less than in matters dealing with
Jews and Gentiles.

Although Paul's advice is clear and unambiguous, his
supporting arguments deserve closer scrutiny. Particularly striking is what Paul does not say. He quotes no saying of Jesus about the status of women, cites no verses from
Scripture, appeals to no fixed natural law. His opening
comments about the hierarchical character of the world
seem less like a natural theology than commonsense obser-
vations about the way the world is. Even the force of his
allusion to the creation story in Genesis 2 ("For man was
not made from woman, but woman from man," I Cor.
11:8–9) is blunted by his balancing statement about how
relationships are now "in the Lord": "Nevertheless, in the
Lord woman is not independent of man nor man of
woman; for as woman was made from man, so man is now
born of woman. And all things are from God" (I Cor. 11:
11–12).

The "nature" to which Paul appeals in vs. 14–15 ("Does
not nature itself teach you that for a man to wear long hair

is degrading to him?") is simply custom ("Everyone knows that men who wear their hair long are . . ."). The conclusion of his argument is a forthright appeal to church practice: Women do not uncover their heads in other churches, so neither should you (v. 16).

The reasons Paul advances for his views are not terribly impressive, and the difference from his mode of argumentation in Galatians is notable. There is no appeal to the "gospel," no detailed interpretation of the Scriptures, no harking back to what had occurred at baptism. His arsenal contains little more than custom and common sense—precisely the sorts of arguments he dismisses in Galatians. In matters dealing with Jews and Gentiles, church practice is irrelevant; what matters is the truth of the gospel. In this instance, Paul behaves more like Peter, whom he attacks for inconsistency in Galatians. He is willing to compromise on the matter of women's rights for the sake of something greater. That "something greater," however, is not a particular understanding of natural law or orders of creation, but order within the congregation.

The survival of the Corinthian congregation was of obvious concern to Paul. As pastor, he was faced with difficult decisions. His congregation was tearing itself apart, and one of the reasons was the activities of women. Here, as elsewhere, the church was divided between the "strong" and the "weak," between those who were ready for liberation and those who were not. The matter was not capable of easy resolution. Women who had removed their veils could appeal with justification to Paul's theology. Others, however, found such radical social behavior intolerable. Their lives were too bound up in the traditional sexual roles. Paul had to decide, with the congregation, if this was an issue for the sake of which to risk the community, the oneness in Christ, that the Corinthians already shared.

Those who seek to make Paul the first apostle of women's liberation overstate the case. There is little evidence in these few verses that he agonized over the matter of women's roles. It would be too much to expect a first-century Christian to advocate equalization of sexual roles or freedom for slaves. Economic conditions made such possibilities totally unrealistic. In a world where Christians were a tiny minority, little could be done to translate "neither male nor female" or "neither slave nor free" into social practice. Problems were far more complex than those involved in breaking down the barriers that separated Jew and Gentile. Paul, in any case, had little desire to play the role of a political or social revolutionary.

Paul's support for the status quo, however, was only provisional. He recognized the need for order and structure within the church. "God is not a God of confusion but of peace." That peace is important. Human beings cannot survive without some order, without structured relationships that communicate a sense of what to expect from others and what others expect in return. Paul most emphatically did not, however, insist upon the eternal validity of one particular social order. He did not attack women in the Corinthian church for alleged violations of God's law. He argued only that their behavior offended common sense—and in this instance, for the sake of peace and order, he was willing to defend common sense.

Understanding Paul's approach is important because it leaves open the possibility for a very different word in another circumstance. To construe Paul's commonsense approach as an appeal to a fixed order of nature according to which wives must be subordinate to husbands is seriously to misunderstand the character of Paul's letter and of his theology. We will have opportunity to consider the family in more detail later. Christians who defend traditional social roles against what they consider threats from radicals are correct when they insist upon the need for order and stability. They are wrong, however, when they appeal to the Bible in defense of one order or structure.

The tendency to absolutize one way of living together—like subordinating women and blacks—as a defense against the dreaded specter of chaos has proved too strong a temptation for most societies and for many Christian traditions as well. Though he had strong opinions about a variety of matters, including the proper role for women in congregations, Paul did not express his views in terms of absolutes. He knew the difference between his opinions and the eternal will of God (I Cor. 7:12, 25, 40). That did not excuse him from having to decide what was the will of God in situations where there were no set answers, but it left open the opportunity for disagreement.

It is not surprising to find small-scale social revolutions in Paul's churches. The gospel he preached had revolutionary implications. The consistent pressure toward equality in Western civilization, resulting first in freedom for slaves, then in voting rights for women, now in calls for complete equality of opportunity for men and women of all races, has been generated at least in part by long-established Christian principles, deeply rooted in our society. It is ironic and sad that some of the strongest opposition to equality for blacks and Hispanics and women has come from churches. Scarcely anything is more basic to the gospel than reconciliation and abrogation of false distinctions that make possible the recovery of our oneness in God.

Paul's advice that women in Corinth submit to the pressures of society is a reminder, however, that the community in which we live out our oneness in Christ provides limits to the exercise of our freedom in the gospel. Our decisions about how we will live as children of God have a bearing on others. It is quite proper that the search for social roles consonant with the gospel should produce tensions. It is improper to expect those tensions to be resolved. The oneness in Christ we experience as members of Christ's body is only provisional, qualified by the reality of alienation in a fallen world. Ultimate reconciliation is

something toward which all reality strains. In the meantime, those who have been baptized into Christ will continue to sense the gulf between the way things will be and
the way they are. The church, living between the times,
can provide a foretaste of what is to come, an alternative
to destructive social patterns.

Decisions about the shape of discipleship thus require
an understanding of how the gospel becomes embodied in
our corporate lives. Like Paul, we must attend to the
needs of the community as well as the "truth" of the gospel. A decision to support the women's movement within
the church as an expression of our true unity in the gospel
makes sense. Society is already far ahead of most churches;
economic conditions make experimentation with social
roles possible. The same decision may not be appropriate
for small churches in other places—for example, in Islamic
countries. Even the removal of veils could be construed as
an attack on society and could occasion violence, perhaps
even the refusal of permission to gather as Christians. The
most committed believers might well disagree about what
constitutes proper testimony to the gospel in such a setting. Knowing the goal of history, we must still live in the
present, relying as did Paul on conventional wisdom and
on hunches in some cases.

Liberation is an enterprise that involves others whose
emotional survival hangs on the delicate balance between
order and novelty. As our society becomes more and more
fragmented, less and less traditional, cries for order and
coherence and stability are becoming louder and louder.
We must attend to those needs as well. Living together as
children of God depends upon a shared system of values.
There will be occasions, however, when we must risk that
unity for the sake of fidelity to the gospel, the power that
alone can bring about real unity. We will have to choose
our issues carefully. Paul had his. For the sake of the unity
of Jew and Gentile he was willing to risk everything. A

church that discriminated against one or the other was, in his view, no church.

To be baptized into Christ means to embrace the new possibilities God has opened to us with all the attendant ambiguities. We live as members of a new community in Christ, and we are called to serve as agents of reconciliation in a fragmented world. Learning how to live together in Christ, in whom there is neither Jew nor Greek, slave nor free, male nor female, is at least part of what it means to "walk worthy of our calling." Knowing how to live as liberated children of God outside the community of the faithful is the topic of the next chapters.

2

CHRISTIANS AND THE WORLD

Put on the whole armor of God, that you may be able to stand against the wiles of the devil. For we are not contending against flesh and blood, but against the principalities, against the powers, against the world rulers of this present darkness, against the spiritual hosts of wickedness in the heavenly places. (Eph. 6:11–12)

The letter to the Ephesians speaks glowingly about life within the new community in Christ. Those who were dead have been made alive; those in darkness have been called into the light. Dividing walls that formerly separated the children of God have now been broken down. Jews and Gentiles live together, experiencing part of the reconciliation between heaven and earth that God destined from the foundation of the world. Christians are called to deal with one another in ways that mirror the relationship between Christ and the church.

Cast in negative terms, these verses from Ephesians 6 call attention to another aspect of the life of faith: members of the church must live in the world. Here, armor and weapons are required. Walking worthy of one's calling will involve encounter with the devil, with principalities and powers, with the world rulers of this present darkness and the spiritual hosts of wickedness in the heavenly places.

The world is pictured as a battleground, the enemy as a force of evil far greater than the sum total of human acts of willfulness.

Such metaphors for describing evil may have lost their power for many of us. While primitive societies seek to understand the world in terms of good and evil powers, we seek to remove the mystery by understanding it in terms of natural processes. We attribute diseases, not to demons, but to bacteria or viruses. Our healing rituals take place in hospitals and laboratories. Our picture of the world has permitted us to exercise a considerable measure of control over our environment—which is why we call ourselves "modern" as opposed to "primitive."

Practitioners of the so-called social sciences have offered comprehensive theories to account for other dimensions of sin and evil. Sociologists speak of the influence of culture; psychologists, of the importance of early childhood experiences; behavioralists, about reinforced patterns of behavior; biologists, about the relationship between hormones, blood chemicals, and personality disorders. If successful, such an approach to life could eliminate the sense of mystery and reduce "principalities and powers" to chemical imbalances or unhealthy cultural patterns.

The mystery of evil remains. There is something irreducibly willful about the human spirit. We hurt one another, not because we have to but because we want to. We know that understanding our problems is helpful in controlling them, but it is not sufficient. The life of faith is a battle with sin, a struggle with a willfulness that we never quite master.

But evil cannot be reduced to individual transgression. The forces against which we struggle do not all arise from within. We may resist believing in demons, but there are aspects of life that cannot be explained by appeal to natural processes any more than by appeal to individual transgression. There is a sense in which life seems to conspire against us. No one may set out to do evil, but the result of the actions of people who are only doing what is expected of them can be destructive. Few of the people I have counseled during my ministry could be described as victims of their own undoing. Most were bruised and broken victims of a world surprised at its own injustice.

Helen was a middle-aged woman whose husband had died unexpectedly. She was unemployed, had no profession or skill. She had never expected to have to earn a salary. She had married early, and she had eagerly chosen to assume responsibility for home and children. After her husband's death, Helen had tried various clerical jobs, but because she could not type well she never lasted more than a month or two. Women at the unemployment office, she said, made her feel cheap for accepting checks, but she had been unable to find a firm willing to train a middle-aged woman for a responsible position. No one set out to do Helen in. Overworked employees at the unemployment office saw her as a typical case and as an addition to their case load; pressured employers could not invest the time or the money to train her. The result was that Helen was driven to despair, her self-confidence gradually stripped away.

Grace was an older woman who lived on Social Security in an old apartment building near the church. She had never married, worked as a secretary all her life, and was now retired on a subsistence income. She had no family and few friends. Her apartment was shabby, but she could afford no better. The area in which she lived was undergoing extensive renewal. Buildings were being refurbished and sold as luxury condominiums. The renewal was a boon to the sagging tax rolls in the city. Grace, however, feared that her landlord would sell the building to developers, in which case she would have to move. She could never afford to buy her apartment. Though her rooms were shabby, she could at least walk to the store and to church.

She could not imagine moving. No one had set out to drive Grace from her familiar surroundings and her church. Urban renewal, in fact, was hailed as a great blessing. For Grace, it was a curse.

Bill and Elaine, members of a suburban parish, announced one day that they were seeking a divorce. The couple were pillars in the congregation. Their problem was not infidelity. They had simply given up on their marriage. Like many of their friends, they had married just after college. Elaine taught for two years before their first child was born. Though intending to return to teaching, she had chosen to wait until her children were in school. The third child was unexpected and altered Elaine's plans, but she was basically satisfied with her role as mother and housewife.

Bill graduated without any idea what he wanted to do with his life. He had been hired by an insurance firm, a job he had not really sought out, and for reasons he never quite understood, he was an instant hit. He attracted the attention of company executives and was transferred to the New York office. He and Elaine purchased a home in Connecticut, and Bill joined the ranks of the commuters.

The young couple were unprepared for the life of New York suburbanites. Bill left for the train at 6:30 A.M. and did not return until 6:30 P.M., exhausted and emotionally drained. Elaine spent most of her day carting the children to activities and taking the youngest to and from nursery school. Her intellectual stimulation came largely from wives with careers who espoused women's liberation. Elaine felt a bit guilty about not working; she winced when people asked politely if she worked "outside the home." She had always assumed she would return to teaching, but with declining enrollments there was little market for new teachers. Always a good student, Elaine knew she could go back to school to prepare for another career. But, like most suburbanites, she and her husband were mortgaged to the hilt. There was no money for schooling or for child care. Bill was sympathetic, but he had little time and energy to invest in the family; it was all he could do to cope with the pressures from the office. Finally, the tensions became too much. Something cracked, and the two young people determined that they could no longer live together. They did not want to separate, they insisted, but they could no longer withstand the relentless pressures seeking to drive them apart.

"If you continue in my word, you are truly my disciples," Jesus said, "and you will know the truth, and the truth will make you free." "We are descendants of Abraham, and have never been in bondage to any one," his audience replied. We know better. We know that we are bound. We are pushed, pulled, and shaped by forces that we do not even understand. What we purchase and the prices we pay are determined by conglomerates with strange names. The Internal Revenue Service determines the percentage of our income that we are free to spend. Our ability to afford homes and automobiles depends upon interest rates established by a mysterious group known as the "Fed." School boards decide how our children will be educated; network executives determine what we will watch on television. The explosion of lobby groups—from the National Rifle Association to Common Cause to Right to Life—mirrors a growing awareness that our private lives are not really private, that our decisions are made within a narrow range of possibilities that are determined by other forces. And those forces are often destructive. Society's casualties—the unemployed, the aging, the divorced—are crippled by insidious powers that operate within systems, powers that we cannot fully comprehend and frequently cannot control. As children of God, we struggle not only against our own stubborn wills and the wills of individual neighbors but against "principalities and powers."

Ephesians speaks of discipleship as preparation for battle against such forces. But how are we to prepare? What can we expect from "the world"? Can the forces of evil be identified and defeated, or are the prospects for success dim? Knowing what it means to live as a Christian must include some sense of what discipleship looks like outside the walls of the church building. New Testament authors sought to answer such questions for their readers. They did not all have the same answers.

In the Gospel of John, the author paints a sobering picture of what the faithful can expect from life. On the one hand, the narrative uses metaphors for Jesus such as bread, water, light, vine, and resurrection. Jesus provides all that is necessary to sustain life. Yet the world is strangely unreceptive. The poetic lines that open the Gospel speak of rejection and darkness as well as of life and light: "The light shines in the darkness, and the darkness has not overcome it [or, grasped it]. . . . The true light that enlightens every man was coming into the world. He was in the world, and the world was made through him, yet the world knew him not. He came to his own home, and his own people received him not" (John 1:5, 9–11).

The irony is pronounced. The Word by which creation came into being cannot get through to some. Darkness persists. It is the refusal of the darkness to accept the light that drives the story on. Those who ought to understand, like the religious leaders, do not; those who do see are the unexpected, like the Samaritan woman and the man born blind. Jesus speaks about himself openly, yet few understand, and those who do are scandalized. Jesus begins his ministry at a wedding feast by changing 120 gallons of water into wine. The feast is spread; there is more than enough for everyone. Yet people refuse to eat and drink.

The life that readers can expect in the world is most clearly enacted in the story of the man born blind (John 9). "I am the light of the world," Jesus says. As light, he comes into the life of a man blind from birth, opening the eyes of one who had formerly known only darkness. As a result of the miracle, however, the life of a whole village is disrupted. Jesus healed on the Sabbath, a problem for observant Jews. The villagers turn to the authorities for advice. The investigation soon takes on the character of an inquisition. The simple blind man is forced to align himself with Jesus and is consequently rejected by his family (John 9: 20–23) and thrown out of the synagogue. His only "crime" was to be healed of his blindness. As the drama unfolds, the blind man comes to see that Jesus is from God, while his interrogators are forced to declare themselves against Jesus. Irrevocably committed to their narrow interpretation of tradition, they have room neither for miracles nor for the miracle worker. Their decision to exclude the blind man seals their fate and reveals their blindness.

The world John sketches is full of ironies. Things are not as they appear. The brightest and best the world can boast, the religious and political leaders, turn out to be enemies of the light, incapable of enlightenment. The world, a place of vivid contrasts and divisions, poses grave dangers for disciples: "If the world hates you, know that it has hated me before it hated you. If you were of the world, the world would love its own; but because you are not of the world, but I chose you out of the world, therefore the world hates you" (John 15:18–19).

John wrote for Jewish Christians who had been thrown out of their homes and synagogues for professing faith in Jesus. No amount of arguing could convince authorities that Jesus was "the way, the truth, and the life." Battle lines had been drawn. Confessing Jesus meant forfeiting a place within the family and being forced to surrender the name "Jew"—which explains why throughout John the term "the Jews" is used for Jesus' enemies.

The Gospel offers hope to the faithful remnant. Jesus provides all that is necessary to sustain life, abundant life.

The darkness cannot overcome the light. The Gospel warns, however, that life will be lived in the midst of death, that few will prove capable of seeing and believing. "The world" as the place of unbelief offers little prospect of change: "I am praying for them; I am not praying for the world but for those whom thou hast given me, for they are thine. . . . Holy Father, keep them in thy name, which thou hast given me, that they may be one, even as we are one. . . . I do not pray that thou shouldst take them out of the world, but that thou shouldst keep them from the evil one" (John 17:9, 11, 15).

At the other end of the spectrum are the Gospel of Luke and the Acts of the Apostles, two works that together represent the most ambitious literary undertaking in the New Testament. The author of these two volumes, which are dedicated to Theophilus, set out to write the history of Christianity from the birth of John the Baptist to Paul's arrival in Rome. Luke's picture of the world in which Jesus and the apostles lived and worked is very different from John's. Luke paints with a whole range of colors; reality as he sees it cannot be captured in blacks and whites. Dualistic imagery is virtually absent. The author is aware that some people do not understand the truth of the gospel, but blindness is not as pervasive, not as rigid a category. Luke's story is more aptly captured by Jesus' seed parables. Beginnings are small and humble, but the plant that springs from the seed will be large enough to afford protection to all (Luke 13:18–19). Trials await the seed, but a bountiful harvest is assured (Luke 8:4–8).

Luke's world is a battleground of opposing forces, but it is open to change. Few are irrevocably committed to error. Conversion is possible. Jesus commissions his followers to preach "repentance and forgiveness" in his name to all nations (Luke 24:46–47). They do, and as simple men are transformed into great orators, lives are changed. Peter's first sermon at Pentecost results in the conversion of thousands (Acts 2). Power flows from the disciples. People are healed, demons silenced. The author is confident that Jesus' emissaries can hold their own in the marketplace. He tells of numerous confrontations between the apostles and competing propagandists, and the results are always clear-cut victories for the faithful (Acts 8:9–24; 13: 4–12; 16:16–18; 19:11–20). Success becomes the decisive criterion by which to evaluate the new movement, as Gamaliel, a prominent leader of the opposition, himself suggests:

> Men of Israel, take care what you do with these men. For before these days Theudas arose, giving himself out to be somebody, and a number of men, about four hundred, joined him; but he was slain and all who followed him were dispersed and came to nothing. After him Judas the Galilean arose in the days of the census and drew away some of the people after him; he also perished, and all who followed him were scattered. So in the present case I tell you, keep away from these men and let them alone; for if this plan or this undertaking is of men, it will fail; but if it is of God, you will not be able to overthrow them. You might even be found opposing God! (Acts 5:35–39)

Such is Luke's philosophy of history. The validity of the religious movement known as "the Way" is demonstrated by its survival and extraordinary spread. Enemies may execute adherents and some of the leaders, but they cannot impede its growth and its triumphant spread to the ends of the earth. The world Luke sketches has room for the new faith; it is an open place, an arena where believers can argue their case, confident that they will receive a hearing. The faithful are invited into a world in which they can feel at home.

The New Testament suggests that the world can be viewed in several different ways. We should accordingly think about an appropriate range of perspectives rather than the "correct" view. Christians who understand the gospel will not see the world in precisely the same way. The Graces, Helens, Elaines, and Bills will find the world an inhospitable place where God is frequently silent and where mysterious forces tear apart and wear down. Others may find such "realism" unrealistic. Two of my seminary professors, for example, were refugees from Eastern Europe who fled the Communists after the Second World War. They knew firsthand the nature of radical evil, but they had found life in the United States so enjoyable, their freedom to teach so overwhelming, and a reasonable salary so attainable that they were totally bewildered by the suspicion and anger of students during the late '60s. "In Communist Europe we could understand such hostility toward the government," they said; "but in America?"

In a classic study entitled *Christ and Culture*, H. Richard Niebuhr identified various ways in which Christians have understood the relationship between faith and the world. By "culture," Niebuhr means the world of habits, ideas, beliefs, and customs, the technical and artistic achievements that humans have imposed on the world of nature. Culture refers to civilization, to the social world we inhabit as members of families, communities, societies, states, and nations. His study is of great help in our thinking through various ways Christians of the past and Christians of today understand the relationship between the world and the church. Though the categories that Niebuhr uses are not meant as pure types, most readers will probably find one of the categories far more congenial than the others.

1. *Christ Against Culture*

The first response is a total rejection of the claims of culture. John's Gospel comes close to representing this view, as does the Apocalypse of John (the book of Revelation). When confessing Jesus meant exclusion from families and synagogues, Christians could appreciate only the contradictory nature of claims made by church and society. Likewise when the Roman government forced a choice between Christ and Caesar, compromise with the state was impossible. For Christians in such circumstances, the world appears polarized between the forces of darkness and the forces of light. No middle ground exists. Loyalty to society or to the state represents a betrayal of loyalty to Christ and his church.

Those who understand the gospel in this way clearly appreciate the negative potential of human culture. In classical biblical terms, sin is the refusal to acknowledge God as God and to substitute an idol. The idol may be the state. At least in the past, in certain Communist countries, church membership involved severe consequences. The state understood the church as a competitor. Citizens had to choose: Christ or culture, Christ or the state. Even in so-called Christian countries of today, believers can identify the corrupting potential of culture. Serious critics of public education point out, for example, that the noble principle of toleration, as understood in American society, militates against particularity and commitment. Toleration comes to mean indifference to specific religious traditions rather than an appreciation of diversity. Leaders in the women's movement point out how effectively sexual stereotypes are reinforced in the classroom. Theologians note how easily natural science takes on religious dimensions, suggesting to students that explanations of things, not values, lie at the heart of the human enterprise. The poor, the aging, the handicapped appreciate the sense in which the whole system of employment and taxation and health care seems to work against retaining a sense of decency and against the formation and maintenance of real community.

One response is to identify culture as the enemy and to withdraw as totally as possible. In the Middle Ages the monastic movement provided an opportunity for such radical rejection of the world. The acceptance of "poverty, chastity, and obedience" was a repudiation of society's institutions and a withdrawal into the community of the holy. Though monastic communities are less attractive as alternatives in present society, they still exist. Other groups, such as the Amish, have proved successful in withdrawing in an organized way from American society, providing their own educational and governmental institutions, satisfying most of their physical needs with a minimum of commerce with the outside world.

Other Christians who may have equally strong feelings about the evils of culture express their opposition in more limited ways. The increase in Christian schools represents a growing dissatisfaction with public education among believers who sense conflict between Christ and culture. Various pacifist movements arise from convictions that any participation in national conflicts represents an impossible compromise with the claims of the gospel. Christians with such a radically negative view of the world believe it to be beyond redemption. They understand their call as directing them away from the corrupting forces of human civilization to a place where righteous living is at least possible.

Such a position is not typical of the vast majority of Christians; it never has been. Critics of separatism point out that even the Amish depend for their survival on the protection of laws, enforced by police and soldiers who are paid by taxes. Soldiers who fought in the Second World War had reason to resent pacifist farmers in the Dakotas who bought up available land while they were away in battle. Further, separatist movements have exerted powerful influences upon society. Amish settlements have impressed neighbors with their virtues of simplicity and hard work. The scholarly and artistic benefits to society from the monastic movements have been enormous, if unintended. Christians who tend in this direction, however,

sense only the negative potential of human culture. For
them, Christ is the eternal opponent of civilization that
seeks to place itself on the throne of God.

2. *The Christ of Culture*

At the other end of the spectrum are believers whose
view of culture is as positive as the former is negative.
"Gee, Reverend," said a parishioner after the Sunday service, "that sermon was great! Just like we hear at the
Masons'!" Carried through consistently, such a view sees
little difference between the claims of the gospel and the
goals of civilization. Christians of this sort might be citizens who are unable to distinguish between "Christian"
and "American," who see the capitalist system as the embodiment of biblical virtues. Niebuhr uses as his example
nineteenth-century Protestant theologians in Europe,
representatives of Christian liberalism. Beginning with
human experience or with contemporary culture, they
sought to show the relevance of the gospel to their age,
translating the faith into categories understandable to
their contemporaries and compatible with the goals of
society.

There are fewer believers of this sort today than there
were in the nineteenth century. Two world wars de-
stroyed liberal Protestant theology in Europe. They illus-
trated graphically the demonic potential of the state, ex-
posing as naive the notion that society was gradually
progressing toward the Kingdom of God. We have become so accustomed to revelations of corruption among
politicians, so suspicious of motives, that even the most
patriotic American will have difficulty identifying the will
of God with the current administration's domestic policy.
"Cultural religion" has been replaced by cultured despis-
ers of religion and religious critics of culture. The visibility
of suffering and corruption in our world, and the lack of
consensus about social and political policies even among

Christians, make a view of the harmonious relationship between Christ and culture appear naive.

3. *Christ Above Culture*

The vast majority of Christians recognize that discipleship necessarily involves life in the world. Theologians point out that the God who graciously forgives sins is also the creator of heaven and earth. Though sin pervades the world, the world is still God's. Further, most Christians understand not only that the world is corrupted but that the assembly of the faithful offers no escape from sin. George Orwell's *Animal Farm* illustrates what we know to be true: today's revolutionaries become tomorrow's conservatives; yesterday's anarchists are today's tyrants. There is no escape from selfishness and tyranny, for we carry their seeds within us. Christians cannot hide from evil by fleeing society. Most Christian tradition falls between the extremes of the separatists and the cultural Christians.

The first of the positions that Niebuhr describes as centrist understands the difference between the claims of Christ's church and the claims of culture but sees no unbridgeable chasm between. There are laws discernible by reasonable people—human laws—that make organized social life possible, just as there are other laws—divine laws—that are not obvious within the created order but that must be revealed by God. The social order is responsible for the one group of laws, the church for the other. The point is that the laws are not contradictory. In the view of Thomas Aquinas, perhaps the greatest theologian in the medieval church, grace was largely a supplement to natural possibilities among human beings, divine laws a supplement to human laws. The church could claim a certain priority to its rules for living—thus theology was described as the "Queen of the Sciences"—but the church could also afford to maintain a very positive relationship with the culture.

This has always been a feature of Roman Catholicism. The ability of the church to coexist with different cultures has been remarkable. Saints in the Mexican Catholic Church have Spanish names; even some of the ancient gods of native Mexican religions have found their way into Catholic tradition in some form. Italian and Polish Catholics have their own indigenous saints and religious culture. Not accidentally, the great artists and composers in such societies have painted and composed for the church.

The great synthesis of medieval Catholicism has gradually broken down, however. Catholic priests in El Salvador and in Poland find themselves pitted against the state, sometimes actively supporting revolution. Dutch bishops have been pressing for major changes in the church based on their cultural heritage. American Catholic women make decisions about family size with less and less concern for the position of the church. As society has changed, the chasm between the church and the world has widened, making it difficult for most moderns to maintain an easy alliance between them. The following two positions seem more typical of Christianity in the modern world.

4. *Christ and Culture in Paradox: Dualists*

Like synthesists, Niebuhr's dualists are aware that the problem facing the human race is not culture, but sin, sin that penetrates everyone and everywhere. They also agree that culture is a gift of God, part of the created order God rules as creator and sustainer. Further, such Christians believe that the place where the elect are called to serve God and neighbor is the world, outside the walls of the sanctuary.

Dualists are aware, however, that there are important differences in the way church and society approach life. One difference is the place of human achievement. Society survives by rewarding virtue and punishing transgression. It understands human beings as capable of both good and evil. Its task is to instill a sense of responsibility for doing good, and to restrain evil. Luther, perhaps the best example of a dualist, understood the importance of what he termed "civil righteousness," human goodness as defined by human laws. Culture "makes men out of wild beasts and prevents men from becoming wild beasts." Luther was, moreover, appreciative of cultural achievements. He was a fine musician and a superb translator and author with enormous respect for the beauty and power of language. Luther had a high view of human potential measured in terms of cultural standards.

As a pastor, however, Luther recognized that society was not religiously neutral. Even at its best, the whole social enterprise conspires to convince people that they are responsible for themselves and their destiny. Society rewards those who give more than it does those who receive; it seeks to create an appreciation for achievement. Those social virtues, however, make it more difficult to accept limitations. In his chilling book *The Denial of Death*, Ernest Becker argues that our culture is a grand attempt to escape from having to face the reality of death. Culture does not lead one to God. It cultivates distaste for a God who gives to those who are undeserving; it stirs rebellion against the God who is the ultimate reminder of our limitedness. By pretending that humans can achieve their destiny, culture leads to despair. Salvation can come only through an alien word, a word of forgiveness and grace from a Savior who died at the hands of a rebellious world. Before God, achievement is worthless. Status is a gift, "apart from works of law."

Luther recognized, on the other hand, that those saved by grace cannot withdraw from the world. They are called to serve God precisely in their ordinary tasks as parents, citizens, and employees. That means living in a world that operates by law, a world that can survive only by rewarding achievement, instilling competition, and punishing sloth and transgression. God's hand can even be seen in that world which is so unaware of his grace. The Creator sustains the world by restraining evil through the rule of law. The law cannot redeem, but it can keep order. Without the law, without threats and punishments, society would disintegrate.

Christians exist simultaneously in two spheres, according to Luther: the realm of the law and the realm of the gospel. God is present in both, but God's action is perceived differently. In the secular realm, God shows an "alien" side, appearing as a God of wrath. God works through threats and rules, through legislatures and law enforcement officials, through systems that reward virtue and feed self-interest. In the church, works count for nothing; in the world, they are essential. Believers thus live as forgiven sinners, whose lives are a gift and whose achievements cannot coerce God into dispensing divine love, and as citizens of a world that will measure performance. The place of law and gospel must not be confused. To be only gracious and forgiving in the world would spell disaster, for without restraint, evil would wreak havoc. To speak of human virtue in any ultimate sense, however, would be to misunderstand the nature of grace.

Luther was conservative socially and politically. On the one hand, he saw no need for profound changes, since the major institutions of his society functioned well. Parents and princes were doing their jobs. Furthermore, though he knew of social and political corruption, he trusted self-confident Christian reformers ("enthusiasts," he called them) less than politicians. He had seen the harm done by a corrupt church in the name of God and feared the unbridled excesses of believers who were as certain as the pope that they knew God's will. He preferred living with imperfections rather than risking fanaticism.

This approach to living in the world is captured in Robert Bolt's *A Man for All Seasons.* In the play, Henry

re and government. They recognize the necessity
tutional structures and their enormous potential for
Moltmann, in his book *The Crucified God,* has gone
s to argue that specific forms of economic organiza-
d government are more Christian than others:
ratic socialism represents in his estimation the
t symbol for the liberation of God's children from
nic and political bondage. Followers of Jesus, called
e God by serving their neighbors, cannot abdicate
sibility for the shape of social and political institu-
nat have such bearing on the shape of individual
lives.

ists will point out, of course, that Moltmann's politi-
ology often appears little more than justification for
rman way of life. Some of his arguments are simply
or, perhaps more fairly, undeveloped. The ade-
of an economic theory would have to be deter-
not simply by appeal to religious principles but by
rkability of the theory. We live in a world in which
theories often fail miserably. Economists confess
ey have only dim perceptions of how the economy
es and little notion of how to control it. The disclo-
ne years ago by the editors of *Forbes* magazine that
selected by throwing darts at the listings in *The
treet Journal* performed several percentage points
than stocks selected by experts only confirms our
on. And there is little reason to suspect that those
dy theology have any deeper insight into the mys-
f economics and politics.

: liberation theologians recognize, however, is the
r battle with the dominant institutions in society.
can be changed, and though Christians are not the
oup concerned with justice, justice is a concern for
ns. It is not enough to offer personal support to
like Helen, Grace, Elaine, and Bill. Women have
led greater opportunity in the business world. Per-

VIII has proposed to divorce his queen and remarry and
has asked the opinion of Sir Thomas More. More knows
that if he opposes the marriage, the king will have him
executed. Yet he cannot condone the marriage as a minister of the church. He has taken refuge in silence, for
until he commits himself, the king cannot legally take
action. In this scene, Sir Thomas' daughter Margaret and
son-in-law William Roper are advising him to arrest a
slippery character named Rich, sent by the king to spy
on More.

MARGARET: Father, that man's bad.
MORE: There is no law against that.
ROPER: There is! God's law!
MORE: Then God can arrest him.
ROPER: Sophistication upon sophistication!
MORE: No, sheer simplicity. The law, Roper, the law. I
    know what's legal, not what's right. And I'll stick to
    what's legal.
ROPER: Then you set man's law above God's!
MORE: No, far below; but let me draw your attention to a
    fact—I'm *not* God. The currents and eddies of right and
    wrong, which you find such plain sailing, I can't navi-
    gate. I'm no voyager. But in the thickets of the law, oh,
    there I'm a forester. I doubt if there's a man alive who
    could follow me there, thank God . . .
ALICE *(pointing after Rich):* While you talk, he's gone!
MORE: And go he should, if he was the Devil himself, until
    he broke the law!
ROPER: So now you'd give the Devil benefit of law!
MORE: Yes. What would you do? Cut a great road through
    the law to get after the Devil?
ROPER: I'd cut down every law in England to do that!
MORE: Oh? And when the last law was down, and the Devil
    turned round on you—where would you hide, Roper,
    the laws all being flat? The country's planted thick with
    laws from coast to coast—man's laws, not God's—and if
    you cut them down—and you're just the man to do it—
    d'you really think you could stand upright in the winds
    that would blow then? Yes, I'd give the Devil benefit of
    law, for my own safety's sake.

ROPER: I have long suspected this; this is the golden calf;
the law's your god.
MORE: Oh, Roper, you're a fool, God's my god. . . . But I
find him rather too subtle . . . I don't know where he is
nor what he wants.
ROPER: My god wants service, to the end and unremitting;
nothing else!
MORE: Are you sure that's God? He sounds like Moloch.
But indeed it may be God—And whoever hunts for me,
Roper, God or Devil, will find me hiding in the thickets
of the law!

5. *Christ as Transformer of Culture*

In a class discussion following a lecture that concluded
with the words from *A Man for All Seasons,* students were
quick to respond: "What about Jews in Germany during
the Second World War? What protection did they find in
the 'thickets of the law'?" Those familiar with the play
pointed out that the king managed to condemn Sir
Thomas in spite of the law. He secured a false confession
from his spy Rich. The forces of evil triumphed despite the
law. Still others observed that the law actually enforces
injustice in some cases. At one time, citizens of the United
States could be punished for aiding runaway slaves. That
was the law of the land.

All those students who felt uncomfortable with the implied social and political conservatism in the dualist position would have felt more at home in Niebuhr's last category. This position, represented in American church
history largely by branches of the Reformed tradition, sees
the dualist assessment of the prospect for improving conditions in the world unduly pessimistic. Luther was willing
to leave the business of government to the princes; Calvin
played an active role in the founding and the governing
of Geneva. Calvin and others in the Reformed tradition
understood the power of evil but placed greater stress on
God's triumph over the principalities and powers and on

his involvement in creation. Th
closest to that of Acts. In seeki
for democracy and in his effor
Nations, Woodrow Wilson embo
vinist religious heritage.

Liberation theologians like J
tavo Gutiérrez are represent
Christian involvement in the
challenge to more traditional
gospel and its implications ar
oppressed—from so-called th
minorities, and from women.
Migliore writes:

> At least since the Enlightenme
> has been increasingly understoo
> for freedom. During this same
> practices of the church have be
> too often justified, attack as bein
> predictable allies of the establis
> ever that happens to be. If Chris
> in a compelling way to people to
> clear that the God of the gosp
> genuine human freedom but is i
> cate.

He adds:

> While there are many differen
> tives of this theology, they are ag
> the struggle for liberation. God
> activity is the ultimate basis an
> by which people break free fror
> Human beings are in bondage r
> ness but also to economic, social,
> world. God wills all people to
> inclusive community character
> ship instead of exploitation and

Liberation theologians have
justice and in proposing altern;

of cul
of inst
good.
so far
tion a
demo
cleare
econo
to ser
respor
tions
huma
Dua
cal the
the G
naive,
quacy
mined
the w
"ideal
that th
operat
sure sc
stocks
Wall
better
suspic
who st
teries
Wha
need f
Societ
only g
Christ
people
dema

haps other Helens will be more adequately prepared for careers or will find training programs to assist them in making transitions to new occupations. Other Graces may find city planners willing to ensure the availability of low-cost housing in renewal projects if Gray Panthers become a political force. Business leaders may be helped to recognize the importance of family stability among employees. Company-sponsored day care centers already offer some assistance in coping with the pressures on two-career families. Christians who view Christ as the transformer of culture recognize advocacy of such changes as features of discipleship, as an outgrowth of concern for the welfare of other children of God.

Christians need not agree on the precise shape of life in the world. We can acknowledge, however, that discipleship will involve engagement with the world and with "principalities and powers," and that such engagement will require both protection and weapons. The New Testament may not solve our problems, but it can call us to battle and fit us for the struggles ahead. In the next several chapters we will examine in more detail specific features of discipleship in the real world.

3

CHRISTIANS AND THE STATE

Be subject to one another out of reverence for Christ. (Eph. 5:21)

An inescapable feature of life in the world is structure. Ephesians speaks of that structure in terms of subjection. Wives, children, and slaves are called to obey those set over them. Though we may disagree with the precise shape of the structure in Ephesians, we can acknowledge the need for some pattern of organization. In our society, corporate life is ordered in the form of constitutional government. A body of laws, enforced by agents of government, makes possible our survival. Most of us sense what it would be like without those laws. In his book *Lord of the Flies,* William Golding offers a chilling glimpse of the dark forces that civilization seeks to restrain. In the story, a group of British children are abandoned on a deserted island. Without sufficient enforcement, their meager attempts at self-government break down. The civilized children revert to savages, and before help arrives two of the youngsters are murdered. A naval officer arrives in time to prevent another execution. "I should have thought that a pack of British boys—you're all British aren't you?—would have been able to put up a better show than that," he says, surveying the incredible scene before him. Under the protection of the adult world—and the British Navy—Ralph, the former leader of the children, reflects on the experience of life in the natural state:

> And in the middle of them, with filthy body, matted hair, and unwiped nose, Ralph wept for the end of innocence, the darkness of man's heart, and the fall through the air of the true, wise friend called Piggy.
> The officer, surrounded by these noises, was moved and a little embarrassed. He turned away to give them time to pull themselves together; and waited, allowing his eyes to rest on the trim cruiser in the distance.

The story ends with the symbol of the warship, a reminder of the harsh reality of life together. Without political structure we would soon tear ourselves to pieces.

Not surprisingly, the New Testament acknowledges the necessity of government and the state. Jesus advises his followers to pay taxes, to "render to Caesar the things that are Caesar's" (Mark 12:13–17). Paul makes a more extended comment to Christians in Rome:

> Let every person be subject to the governing authorities. For there is no authority except from God, and those that exist have been instituted by God. Therefore he who resists the authorities resists what God has appointed, and those who resist will incur judgment. For rulers are not a terror to good conduct, but to bad. . . . Pay all of them their dues, taxes to whom taxes are due, revenue to whom revenue is due, respect to whom respect is due, honor to whom honor is due. (Rom. 13:1–3,7)

Some interpreters of Romans through the centuries have taken the passage to be a blanket approval of governmental authority. The verses are remarkably terse, however. They attempt nothing like a complete political theory, grounding governmental structures in a detailed picture of cosmic organization. Christians are advised to respect the authorities of government, perhaps to head off tendencies to abandon political and social responsibilities now that they had become "new creations" in Christ. Paul suggests little more than that believers must live out their faith in the world, where cooperation with others is necessary. At the very least, the state makes cooperation possible. The alternative, anarchy, is as distasteful to Christians as to the authorities, since God "is not a God of confusion, but of peace" (I Cor. 14:33).

Such political advice is largely common sense and can be found in virtually identical wording in non-Christian moralists. Paul does not suggest that Christians ought to become political leaders, nor that political leaders need to be Christians. The job of the state is to dispense justice. There is no hint in these verses that the state is in any sense the embodiment of the Kingdom of God or that it is intended to lead men and women to Christ. Its purpose is to keep order and ensure peace. Because God is the creator and sustainer of the world, his will can be seen, however imperfectly, in the exercise of governing authority.

What happens, however, when the state is hostile to the gospel or when rulers do not reward the righteous and punish the wicked? Paul did not even deal with the question, but John, the author of the Apocalypse, did. The visionary work was composed toward the end of the first century, probably under the reign of Domitian (81–96 A.D.). The Apocalypse stands in a tradition of visionary literature known as "apocalyptic" (from the Greek "to reveal"), including such works as Daniel and intertestamental books such as I Enoch, IV Ezra, II Baruch, and others. John drew heavily on Daniel, which was written during the persecution of Jews under the Syrian ruler Antiochus IV. Antiochus made observing the Commandments a capital offense. Daniel was written for beleaguered Jews whose very survival was in question. Like Daniel, John's Apocalypse is resistance literature, composed for a troubled remnant for whom the world had become a threatening place.

In the Apocalypse, the state is evil. Terrible beasts symbolize past and current rulers. The bizarre imagery is a thinly veiled reference to contemporary rulers and events. The beast with seven heads and ten horns (ch. 13) symbolizes Rome, with its succession of emperors (see also the vision in ch. 17):

> And I saw a beast rising out of the sea, with ten horns and seven heads, with ten diadems upon its horns and a blasphemous name upon its heads. . . . And to it the dragon gave his power and his throne and great authority. . . . Men worshiped the dragon, for he had given his authority to the beast, and they worshiped the beast, saying, "Who is like the beast, and who can fight against it?" And the beast was given a mouth uttering haughty and blasphemous words, and it was allowed to exercise authority for forty-two months. . . . Also it was allowed to make war on the saints and to conquer them. And authority was given it over every tribe and people and tongue and nation. (Rev. 13:1–2, 4–5, 7)

The government of Rome, says the vision, receives its authority from the prince of evil. Rulers may not be completely outside the will of God, since the devil operates with God's permission. But Christians are not obliged to cooperate with the government for that reason. What they can expect from the state is trouble. Professing faith in God and the Lamb will incur the wrath of rulers. Government is still the agency of law and order, but now the whole enterprise serves to prevent true worship of God. John calls the faithful not to obey rulers but to endure them, confident that in the end God will destroy them.

Contemporary Christianity operates within the same two poles. We speak of government as an "order of creation," locating the state within a structure of divine law. Yet some of the most conservative Protestant traditions with the highest respect for divine law are among the most vocal opponents of cooperation with Communist governments. The state, they recognize, even if deriving its authority from God, can become demonic—or at least corrupt.

There is not one "Christian" view of the state in contemporary Christendom. That is hardly surprising, considering the variety of governments under whose rule Christians live and the wide range of views about what constitutes proper governmental policy among churches. To get some sense of the range, it might be useful to examine various attitudes in the light of Niebuhr's categories discussed in Chapter 2.

1. *Christ Against Culture: The State as Evil*

Among some Christian traditions in this country there is a deep-seated suspicion of government. Sometimes it is expressed in the sentiment that "politics is a dirty business." In other cases, the suspicion is translated into policy. Jehovah's Witnesses view loyalty to the state as religiously objectionable; a pledge of allegiance to the flag constitutes idolatry. The most obvious target of such suspicion are anti-Christian governments. Many with a fondness for John's Apocalypse have sought to identify the Soviet Union with one of the many beasts. Hal Lindsey, in his best-seller *The Late Great Planet Earth*, views with suspicion virtually all governmental cooperation. The European Common Market, he believes, is a precursor of the government symbolized by the beast with ten heads in Revelation 13:

> If the formation of the European Common Market were an isolated development in the line of Biblical prophecy, then it would have no significance for our study. However, combined with the other pieces of the prophetic puzzle which we are attempting to develop for you, it takes on immense importance.
>
> We believe that the Common Market and the trend toward unification of Europe may well be the beginning of the

ten-nation confederacy predicted by Daniel and the Book of Revelation.

Students of Revelation do not always look beyond the shores of the United States, nor into the future, for application. They are not always conservative Christians. William Stringfellow, in a passionate book entitled *Conscience and Obedience,* concludes with a "Homily on the Significance of the Defeat of the Saints" (Rev. 13:7). Reflecting on his involvement with the Berrigan brothers in the antiwar movement, he offers little hope of significantly changing government. Christians, he insists, even in the United States, are called to oppose the beast and its blasphemous policies:

> For the time being, in the era of the fall, until the consummation of this history in the judgment of the Word of God, the beast knows success and indulges victory; the saints suffer aggression and know defeat. Surely the text (Rev. 13:7) mocks every effort, undertaken in the name of the Christian witness in this world, which is informed by calculations about effectiveness, progress, approval, acclaim—or any of the varieties of success. . . . The churches and, within them, both social activists and private pietists, are virtually incorrigible—despite the admonition of Revelation 13:7—in practicing some such deliberation before risking any putative witness.
> Revelation 13:7 contains no melancholy message. It authorizes hope for the saints . . . enabling the church—as the first beneficiary of the resurrection—to confront the full and awesome militancy of the power of death incarnate in the ruling principalities.

Stringfellow's view of government, including the government of the United States, is largely mirrored in *Sojourners,* a monthly published by a group of Christians concerned to offer a clear testimony to the gospel in contemporary society. In an editorial on the imposition of martial law in Poland, James E. Wallis, the editor, commented:

I have a hard time believing that the U.S. government really
cares any more for the Poles than it does for the Salvador-
ans, or that the Soviet regime is any more seriously concerned about Central American farmers or Afghan villagers. But Christians must care about them all.

We can expect the superpowers to slaughter the innocents then attack each other for doing so. But we must
refuse to take sides in this horrible and deadly hypocrisy.
The innocents cry out in Polish, Spanish, and every other
language. The Herods never hear. But we do, and we must
listen with our whole hearts.

While recognizing the necessity of some governmental
agency, these "radical Christians," as Niebuhr terms
them, are most impressed by the harm done by the state
and the need to offer a prophetic critique of its performance. To use the words of Jim Wallis, "The best unions, like
the best churches, are always a challenge to their governments."

2. *Christ and Culture in Paradox: The State as Necessary in a Fallen World*

Dualists, as Niebuhr terms them, tend to be more cautious in their critique of government. Like Luther and
Paul, they are impressed by the necessity for order. When
Luther believed the state was threatened by the Peasants'
Revolt, he urged its brutal suppression by the military. He
considered repression in this case preferable to chaos.
Reinhold Niebuhr, Richard's brother, was a prominent
advocate of Christian "realism," i.e., the ability to recognize the political compromises necessary for survival in a
world infected by sin. He insisted upon distinguishing
love, the ethical ideal for individuals, from justice, the
ethical goal for society:

> The Christian utopians think they can dispense with all
> structures and rules of justice simply by fulfilling the law of
> love. They do not realize that the law of love stands on the
> edge of history and not in history, that it represents an

ultimate and not an immediate possibility. They think they might usher in the Kingdom of God if only they could persuade men not to resist tyranny and thus avoid conflict. They do not recognize to what degree justice in a sinful world is actually maintained by a tension of competitive forces, which is always in danger of degenerating into overt conflict, but without which there would be only the despotic peace of the subordination of the will of the weak to the will of the strong.

Reinhold Niebuhr sought to encourage support of and participation in government by citizens while also recognizing the limited goals of political organization. Christians, he insisted, cannot be paralyzed by moral ambiguities.

During the Second World War, for example, the United States fought with Communist Russia against Hitler. Our government actively supported Stalin and his war effort, a ruler whose brutality perhaps exceeded that of Hitler and whose political philosophy demanded opposition to the Christian church. During the war years, however, it seemed wiser to fight against Hitler, the more acute threat, than against Stalin. Historians may debate the wisdom of political leaders at the time, but in the early 1940s decisions had to be made. Neither alternative could be termed more Christian than the other. Christian statesmen were forced to debate the issues in terms of limited objectives: Which of two evils was the more dangerous and pressing? The support of the war effort by most churches indicated their awareness that in a fallen world Christians must often make choices between unacceptable alternatives. Dualists respect the ambiguity, insisting on the one hand that the state is necessary, and on the other that its goals are often limited to restraining evil rather than embodying God's law in the world.

Such morally difficult questions abound in our present situation. In the last several years churches have debated the wisdom of divestiture in South Africa. Christian churches have substantial holdings in corporations involved in the South African economy. The government of South Africa recognizes apartheid as official policy. Discrimination against blacks is embedded in the law. What should Christians think of South Africa? On the one hand, apartheid seems clearly to contradict the gospel that "in Christ there is neither Jew nor Greek." On the other hand, South Africa is militantly anti-Communist, and thus a valuable ally in Africa. On the one hand, withdrawal of investments may pressure South African officials to change government policy toward blacks; on the other, the resulting unemployment may harm black workers more than white government officials and drive off an important ally in the struggle against Soviet expansion. The issue has been debated heatedly—with Christians on both sides. Arguments helpful to Christians will focus on political and social realities less than on the law of God. In matters of strategy, dualists argue, there is usually no divine blueprint by which to determine the proper action.

Attitude toward Islamic states is an even more perplexing problem. In Saudi Arabia, conversion to Christianity is a capital offense. The government is consciously opposed to the gospel and to its adherents. The state seems a good candidate for the beast in John's Apocalypse. On the other hand, the Saudi government has been the most favorably disposed of the Arab governments to the United States. It has supplied our industries and the industries of the West with oil and has exercised restraint on price increases. The government has been a moderating influence in the volatile Arab world and an ally against Soviet expansion. Christians can hardly regard the government as ideal—but, dualists would argue, it is better than some alternatives. The Saudi royal family is an important force for peace. Thus even Christians may support in a limited way a government that is totally opposed to Christ and his church; they may in fact see the hand of God in its rule. Politics has to do with what is possible; its goals and expectations are limited.

3. *Christ the Transformer of Culture: The State as a Potential Force for Justice in the World*

In his now-famous book *Theology of Hope,* Jürgen Moltmann offered his critique of a society and a church that had accepted a comfortable separation. Speaking eloquently of moral ambiguities and the need to compromise in the interest of survival, Christians have simply withdrawn from politics. Or perhaps more accurately, they have severed the connection between the gospel and the world in which they live, banishing God from society and politics:

> The divine in the sense of the transcendent has disappeared from the world of nature, of history, and of society. The world has become the material for technical reshaping by man. The gods of cosmological metaphysics are dead. The world no longer offers man a hope and an abiding shelter.

When the gospel relates only to individuals and to their self-perception, whole areas of life come to be viewed as autonomous, as operating according to their own laws; the church, Moltmann argues, then becomes a hospital where people chewed to pieces during the week can come for healing. Why, he asks, should we assume that things must be as they are? If government operates as God's regent, there should be some accountability. And to speak of the church's role only in terms of critique is to ignore the openness of history and of our society. Governmental policy does not change quickly, but it does change. Frequently, those policy shifts are responses to public pressure. Involvement in politics requires stamina, patience, intelligence, and a willingness to compromise; it may even entail involvement in supporting unjust policies. It is not a foregone conclusion, however, that the saints in politics will be defeated.

In a baccalaureate address to graduating seniors at Yale University in 1970, Kingman Brewster, then president, reviewed the recent history of American politics to illustrate the potential for healthy change in our system. He identified several individual citizens whose dogged commitment to causes had resulted in significant policy changes. His examples were Ralph Nader, John Gardner of Common Cause, and William Sloan Coffin, who was at that time chaplain at Yale and under indictment by the Federal Government for activities in opposition to the war in Vietnam. The point of Brewster's address was that cynicism among Christians is unjustified. National policies can be changed. And as civil rights leaders recognized long ago, a voting rights bill can do more to secure justice for outsiders in our society than all the private acts of charity combined.

The message has not been lost on churches. In the last decade in particular, a large number of special-interest groups have formed among Christians who recognize the potential for change in national policy and their responsibility for the shape of that policy. Groups opposed to abortion have organized under the banner of the Right to Life movement and have pressed individual candidates to take a stand on the issue. A loosely organized group known as the Moral Majority, headed by prominent television evangelists, has set out to remove from office candidates whose voting records suggest indifference to religious values. Clergy and Laity Concerned, together with several denominations, have sought to press for disarmament. Even Billy Graham, who as a Baptist has adhered to the principle of separation between church and state, has begun to speak passionately about the need for a less strident foreign policy. Despite their pessimism about government, some members of Sojourners, like Charles Colson, have begun to advocate reform of the prison system. All these groups, and many more, have sought to change national policy by appeal to the law of God. None would deny the need for compromise in the political arena, but neither do they accept present leadership and policy as inevitable.

The prophetic role has always been a difficult one; it is no easier today. It entails great risks. How do we know, for example, that Amos had a firm grasp of the situation in Israel when he issued his scathing indictments against the king and Israelite society in the name of God? Amos' contemporaries did not believe that he spoke for God, and they probably doubted the validity of his analysis. Religious reformers often tend to simplify complex issues, implying that there can be only one "Christian" view on a given issue. The rhetoric has become so inflamed in discussions of abortion oɪ divestiture in South Africa that there can be little genuine conversation. Wayne Booth is perhaps correct: we do not seek to offer sound reasons for our views, because we are convinced that no one on the other side will be persuaded. The political arena thus provides a forum for a test of strength between competing groups of Christians, with one side arguing for the Right to Life and the other arguing for the rights of women and of the poor. It is unlikely that clergy and theologians will settle such struggles without the help of laity who know how things are in the world as well as how they should be, and without the aid of politicians who practice the art of compromise.

The age of great Christian statesmen is probably past. Our society is too diverse and fragmented to sustain a consensus even regarding matters of justice. Tensions between unions and management, men and women, blacks and whites, and capitalists and communists show no signs of abating. There may be a momentary consensus on single issues, but there are few signs of basic agreement on matters of national policy.

That should not be a reason for Christians to withdraw from politics, however. Even separatists insist that political authority is derived from God and that our religious heritage continues to provide a basis for critique of the state. If our government remains open to reform, individual Christians and special-interest groups and whole denominations will continue to press for a more just system of rule and for policies more conducive to peace. Whatever the limitations imposed by the structures of our society, those committed to serve the neighbor can do no less.

4

VOCATION AND OCCUPATION

But grace was given to each of us according to the measure
of Christ's gift. . . . And his gifts were that some should be
apostles, some prophets, some evangelists, some pastors and
teachers, to equip the saints for the work of ministry, for
building up the body of Christ. (Eph. 4:7, 11–12)

I have a young friend in our congregation who is per-
plexed about vocation. He has a good job, enjoys his work,
but has little notion how his faith relates to his job. He once
considered becoming a pastor but decided upon journal-
ism instead. He is bright, competitive, aggressive, the sort
of person who will succeed at whatever he tries. He is also
aware of the pitfalls of success, sober about the seductive-
ness of wealth and position, and deeply troubled by economic injustices built into our system. He is also dismayed
about how little help the church has offered to enable him
to understand what discipleship means for him. "What I
have learned from the church," he told me, "is that there
is something vaguely evil about making money, and that
if you really want to be a Christian, you should become a
pastor."

Whether intentionally or not, churches communicate
such messages. There were two ordinations recently in
our congregation. The services were impressive and mov-

ing. The image of a group of people standing around the candidates with hands on their heads nicely symbolized the community support the young candidates could count on—as well as God's blessing of their ministries. The absence of similar rites for others in the congregation is striking. Installation services for church school teachers or church officers pale by comparison. And there is no rite at all to celebrate the beginning of a career in sales or in teaching, no formal way of invoking God's blessing on other kinds of work. It is as if God's blessing and congregational support were reserved for church work.

Laypeople get the message. When I travel, I try not to tell people too quickly what I do. When they learn that I am a pastor, they usually shift the conversation to relatives who have been pastors or to their experience as choir members or church school teachers. They expect that I will be interested in the church since I am a religious professional, and they seem to see little connection between religion and what they do for a living. I was having a marvelous conversation with a banker on a flight to Sioux Falls. His eyes flashed as he explained to me how important it was for banks to guarantee the financial integrity of their customers to businesses in the community. He was genuinely angry as he described the practices of large banking corporations whose sole concern was to get people to open accounts. The moment he discovered that I was a pastor, however, he began to talk about his church. In spite of Protestant rhetoric about the priesthood of believers and lay ministry and the many volumes written on the topic, most people understand religion to be confined to the church and see little connection with the way they make their living.

Passages like the one from Ephesians are of little immediate help in making the connection between the call of God and employment; in fact, they seem to heighten the problem. Paul's discussion of "gifts" in I Corinthians 12 and in Romans 12 likewise focuses on endowments for the ministry of Christ's body, the church. Such passages testify to the importance of the Christian community in the lives of first-century believers, but they stop short of offering a full-blown understanding of vocation. There are many reasons for the focus on churchly matters. For one thing, Paul's letters were written to churches and dealt with specific congregational problems. He did not intend them to be thorough expositions of faith or discipleship. Furthermore, Paul wrote to people who, like himself, believed there was not much time left before Christ's return.

> I mean, brethren, the appointed time has grown very short; from now on, let those who have wives live as though they had none, and those who mourn as though they were not mourning . . . and those who buy as though they had no goods, and those who deal with the world as though they had no dealings with it. (I Cor. 7:29–31)

Given such expectations, extended discussions about employment would have seemed out of place.

We can nevertheless find some help in thinking about vocation and employment even from Paul's letters. It is significant that when Paul speaks about work, it is in quite ordinary ways:

> But we exhort you, brethren, . . . to aspire to live quietly, to mind your own affairs, and to work with your hands, as we charged you; so that you may command the respect of outsiders, and be dependent on nobody. (I Thess. 4:10–12)

> Now we command you, brethren, in the name of our Lord Jesus Christ, that you keep away from any brother who is living in idleness and not in accord with the tradition that you received from us. For you yourselves know how you ought to imitate us; we were not idle when we were with you, we did not eat any one's bread without paying, but with toil and labor we worked night and day, that we might not burden any of you. . . . If any one will not work, let him not eat. For we hear that some of you are living in idleness, mere busybodies, not doing any work. Now such persons we

command and exhort in the Lord Jesus Christ to do their work in quietness and to earn their own living. (II Thess. 3:6–12)

Paul refers to work as a necessity. There are things people must do to live. Conversion provides no escape from such necessities. It was important, Paul believed, that others get the right impression about Christians. They are not freeloaders, purchasing their newfound freedom at the expense of others.

Notably absent are glowing descriptions of labor. Earning a living involved considerable drudgery for most people. Most philosophers despised skilled labor, Paul's occupation, because it left little time for developing the mind. Paul's recommendation that his converts, largely urban poor, imitate him in working with their hands (i.e., working at a trade) was no invitation to an easy life. As Ronald Hock reminds us,

> Making tents meant rising before dawn, toiling until sunset with leather, knives, and awls, and accepting the various social stigmas and humiliations that were part of the artisan's lot, not to mention poverty—being cold, hungry, and poorly clothed.

Paul advised the Thessalonians to work at a trade, both to avoid idleness—a concern of other moralists of Paul's time—and to achieve a measure of independence. His admonition, "Live quietly and mind your own affairs" was advice to avoid public life. Paul did not assume that his parishioners would amass great wealth or would rise to positions of prominence in the world. He could assume that their impact on the shape of social, political, and economic life would be minimal. And in the light of the imminent close of the age, that was not a matter of great concern.

Paul did not speak glowingly about employment, but neither did he speak of it with contempt. He understood work to be a feature of normal life. His commonsense view typifies the whole Bible. Even paradise includes work as an aspect of life. When Genesis describes the ideal state of people, it includes tasks as an essential ingredient: "The LORD God took the man and put him in the garden of Eden to till it and keep it" (Gen. 2:15). In an ideal world, humans would all be gardeners or farmers. Work, like food and companionship, is essential to life.

We can understand the positive aspects of employment better than could Paul and his contemporaries. Work is necessary as a means of providing food and shelter. But it also offers a channel for creative expression. And the types of employment possible today are considerably more varied than they were in the first century. If Christians are called to serve God and neighbor, employment in our society offers concrete opportunities. Researchers can unlock secrets that eliminate debilitating diseases. By varying housing patterns, city planners can do more to increase interaction among social classes than any amount of school busing. Teachers can open the minds of young people to a world they have never seen. American farmers have the capacity to feed the hungry far beyond our national borders. On a smaller scale, all of us know a mechanic whose good work and honesty renew our faith in the human race, or a dental hygienist whose cheerful disposition can make even a visit to the dentist seem pleasurable. The banker I met on the plane came alive when he spoke about his work. It offered him an opportunity to make the world a better place.

The Bible says more about work, however, than that it is good. The creation story also reminds us that things are not as they were intended to be. None of us lives in the ideal state. Work is a feature of ordinary life, but that life has been poisoned by sin and evil. Labor is not exempted from the effects of the poison:

Cursed is the ground because of you; in toil you shall eat of it all the days of your life; thorns and thistles it shall bring forth to you; and you shall eat the plants of the field. In the sweat of your face you shall eat bread till you return to the ground, for out of it you were taken; you are dust, and to dust you shall return. (Gen. 3:17–19)

Farming is toil, not pleasure. People must work at tasks that are often boring or demeaning. Employment in a fallen world is tied to status; competition and jealousies add unwanted pressures. Talent and hard work are not always rewarded. Women, blacks, and Hispanics suffer from discrimination. "I always thought I enjoyed my work," a recently retired plant manager told me, "but now I can't believe how much better I feel in the morning when I realize that I don't have to take any guff from my boss or listen to the guys complain."

A friend who teaches at a university was explaining to me how complicated life had become for researchers because of government regulations. Because humane societies had complained about maltreatment of laboratory animals, stiff requirements had been imposed on the raising and treatment of laboratory animals. As a result, the university now pays between $1.50 and $4.00 for every mouse it uses in experiments. My friend acknowledged that some regulations were necessary, given the willingness of some colleagues to treat animals cruelly. But there seemed to be no way of achieving moderation once regulators began their work. "Think how simple our work would be if we could trust one another," he mused.

His observation set off a whole train of thought. We cannot trust one another, so our lives are complicated. Ironically, however, that lack of trust provides numerous employment opportunities. Lawyers come to mind first. Our society requires lawyers both to formulate laws for the protection of citizens and to protect citizens against the laws. Lawyers are employed by individuals and corporations to find ways around the law. Laws and regulations thus become more complicated, requiring more legal experts. We need auditors and accountants to keep tabs on merchants and employees; neither can trust the other. The military is the largest single employer within the Federal Government, followed closely by the Internal Revenue Service. Soldiers and tax checkers are necessary because we cannot trust one another to share the burden of government equally and because we need protection against one another. To ensure a fair exchange of goods, we need shopkeepers and bankers. Our lives would indeed be simpler if we could trust one another—but a substantial proportion of the work force would be unemployed! Our economic structure is in large measure a response to the reality of sin.

Jobs are not immediately in jeopardy, of course. The air we breathe is poisoned, so we will continue to require air pollution controllers as well as police, soldiers, lawyers, manufacturers of weapons, shopkeepers, and bankers. Reality demands that we temper traditional Protestant rhetoric about the blessings of labor. Employment is an essential feature of human life, but it is not an unmixed blessing. Labor involves us in a world that is at war with God and with itself, a world under the power of sin. In such a world, Christians may find themselves working in defense-related industries, producing weapons capable of devastating the earth—or supporting such industries through taxes. Though called to be peacemakers, believers can recognize the need for the means to defend against tyranny—while also recognizing the dangerous logic of the arms race. Few are exempted from involvement in such moral ambiguities. Most physicians will acknowledge the injustice of health care programs that invest more and more time and money in expensive procedures and equipment that benefit fewer and fewer people. Liver transplants boast spectacular success, but the surgery requires a team of eight specialists, costs $60,000 per transplant, and benefits a handful of people annually. Most of our health care resources serve the wealthy or those who are insured.

As Christians, we cannot afford to be naive or unduly romantic about labor. There are occupations that are stimulating and that offer opportunity for service and creativity. But no job is free from tensions; every job involves compromises with what we know to be right and just. Work is necessary to life, but some work destroys life, and all work involves us in a system that is more life-giving to some than to others.

What has our employment to do with our call to "walk as children of the light"? Many have found it helpful to distinguish aspects of that call. The commandments to "love one another" or to offer one's enemy the other cheek are appropriate for some settings and inappropriate for others. The way we ought to treat others may differ from one setting to another. Let me give an example.

In a little book entitled *Christianity and Real Life*, William Diehl describes a difficult personnel problem he had to solve as sales manager for Bethlehem Steel Corporation. He had to deal with a salesman named Doug who had been with the company for twenty-two years. Doug had been hired and regularly promoted by people who liked him but who had recognized from the beginning that he lacked the intellectual capacity for managerial positions. He was hardworking and loyal, however, and his employers sought to reward his efforts with promotions. He had finally been elevated to a position he could not handle. More competent employees worked under him. Sales were suffering and staff morale was low. The sales manager had to remove Doug from his position before he did serious damage.

In his book Diehl discusses his dilemma as a Christian in this situation. He was concerned about Doug as a fellow human being, as well as about his wife and children who depended upon him for support. He knew that Doug was probably too old to begin a totally new career. Yet as a Christian, Diehl was obligated not only to do the loving thing for Doug. He had other responsibilities. He was acting on behalf of others who deserved justice. He could not escape from his responsibilities to the corporation, nor could he ignore his responsibilities to Doug as a child of God. The solution Diehl settled on—demoting Doug without a decrease in pay—satisfied no one completely. Doug was hurt by the demotion, the corporation was paying more than necessary for an employee at Doug's level, and Doug's fellow employees resented the exception. In this instance, the institutional setting imposed conditions on the one who had to make a decision about Doug.

One response to such realities, typical of those Richard Niebuhr terms "radical Christians," is to avoid involvement in society's economic institutions. Such Christians understand the degree to which sin infects the working of corporations as well as the rest of secular culture. They understand Amos' scathing indictment of his society and his pronouncement that God would have to tear Israelite society to the ground in order to achieve justice. The systems of culture are poisoned.

Such radical Christians may choose to form their own economic systems, refusing cooperation with secular society. Such believers are few in number but highly visible. The Amish have been the most successful in achieving independence, while followers of Rev. Sun Myung Moon and groups of Jesus People have enjoyed more moderate success. The largely agricultural communities of Amish in Pennsylvania and in Iowa provide most of what those people need for themselves by cultivating simple expectations and life-styles. Instilling a spirit of cooperation rather than competition and gratefulness for simple things rather than an insatiable appetite for more, they seek to avoid the evils and the moral dilemmas of corporate and professional life. Antibusiness sentiments are shared by other people in society whose response is less organized but who are agreed that practicing true vocation is possible only by refusing to participate in corrupt economic institutions.

Those within the business community readily point out that such radical movements are possible only with the support of the larger society. Even the most self-sufficient Amish settlements purchase some manufactured goods. And even the most ardent separatists rely on financial support from the economic institutions of society for police forces that keep the peace and military organizations that defend the country against attack. Such groups do not represent a practical alternative to involvement in the world. Their presence provides a reminder of the radical claims of the gospel for a society that easily disguises its failings and injustices, but if everyone followed the example of those groups and withdrew, society would collapse.

Most churches understand the need to live in the world, if not of the world. For most of us, serving God and our neighbors requires employment, whether as teachers, dentists, or plumbers. It is helpful to recognize, however, that the manner of serving God and the neighbor through jobs requires a different ethic than serving on a private level. Luther, a representative of Niebuhr's "dualists," understood the tension. He spoke glowingly on the one hand about the sacredness of so-called secular vocations and the ability of Christians to serve God through ordinary work:

> If you are a craftsman you will find the Bible placed in your workshop, in your hands, in your heart; it teaches and preaches how you ought to treat your neighbor. Only look at your tools, your needle, your thimble, your beer barrel, your articles of trade, your scales, your measures, and you will find this saying written on them. You will not be able to look anywhere where it does not strike your eyes. None of the things with which you deal daily are too trifling to tell

you this incessantly, if you are but willing to hear it; and there is no lack of such preaching, for you have as many preachers as there are transactions, commodities, tools, and other implements in your house and estate; and they shout this to your face, "My dear, use me toward your neighbor as you would want him to act toward you with that which is his." (In Gustaf Wingren, *Luther on Vocation*)

Luther believed that God the creator was at work in the world as well as within the church. But God's manner of involvement in the world was different. His "strange work" was to resist evil, making life possible. Service to God in the world is thus appropriately different from service to God within the church. Luther could advise Christians that

this is the answer to the question, "How can a Christian bear the sword, since he is supposed to love everybody?" The Christian does not need the sword for his own sake and not for the sake of the other Christians either . . . but it is needed for the sake of evil men. Since they must be stopped and the godly protected, a Christian, if he is called by God and by those who stand in God's stead, may go and kill like the others. (In George Forell, *Faith Active in Love*)

Business ethics for individual Christians must take seriously the condition of the world in which service is rendered. If people in sales must compete to stay in business, Christians will have to compete—unless they choose another occupation. Discipleship on the job is the art of the possible. A young man spoke to a group of pastors about his own moral dilemmas on the job, pastors from whose pulpits he had heard numerous injunctions to deal honestly with others. He had been employed as an architect by a major corporation and had been promoted quickly to a responsible position. One of his chief tasks was to prepare cost analyses for building projects. Costs were broken down into capital expenditures and program expenditures. Program expenses could be deducted from taxes, so the corporation executives were anxious that as many of the costs as possible appear on that side of the ledger. The young man was aware that every corporation operated with the same concern and that economic survival depended upon such practices. He was troubled, however, when his supervisors sent back cost projections with the comment that capital expenditures were too high. Not only was he required to pad program expenditures; he was made legally responsible for the estimates. As a recently employed member of the firm, he could expect to do little to alter company policy. What does it mean to be a faithful servant of God in this setting? he asked the group of pastors.

Luther was not at all hesitant about participating in a world that frequently forced choices between equally unacceptable alternatives. There is a robustness about his "sin boldly" that can be liberating for those constantly impaled on the horns of moral dilemmas. Sin is a condition of human life. We can live as forgiven sinners, however. God's justifying grace can enable us to tolerate the ambiguities, Luther argued, until God chooses to bring history to a close. Christians can learn to live with things as they are.

One problem with such tolerance of ambiguity is that it can lead to complete passivity in social matters. Paul and his contemporaries may perhaps be excused for not attacking boldly the evils of society, for they had little power. For many Christians in American society, that is not true. Niebuhr's distinction between dualists and conversionists is helpful here. We live in different spheres, requiring different moral strategies, but the God who is involved in both is the same God. And the goal of God's involvement in human affairs is not simply the salvation of individual souls but the redemption of all creation. Service to that God may involve a call to change institutions that are unjust; it may instill a restlessness with things as they are.

A Presbyterian pastor told of a parishioner who came to him for advice. As in the preceding story, he had been hired by a large corporation and had risen spectacularly through the ranks. He discovered an aspect of his job that troubled him, however. His company had one of the finest pension plans in the industry—on paper. In practice, when employees neared retirement age, the company made life so difficult for them that most of them quit, forfeiting at least some of their retirement benefits. As a junior officer in the company, the young executive was expected to enforce a policy he knew to be immoral and probably illegal.

The anguished parishioner had come to his pastor for advice. He took seriously his call to serve God and his neighbors. He believed his job made that impossible, and he had decided to quit to protest an immoral policy. "Don't resign," his pastor advised. "Stay with the company until you become president and can change the policy for good." He took his pastor's advice—and when he became president some years later, the shameful practice was abolished.

That pastor understood the potential for good within culture. He recognized the conflict between private morality and corporate realities, but he advised moral compromise in the light of the greater good that was possible by change from within. On the way to his ultimate goal, the officer undoubtedly had to sacrifice many individuals nearing retirement for the sake of his career. Because he had the courage to endure the immorality, he was able to effect a change far greater than he could have accomplished by resigning.

For every such success, there are hundreds of officials who are never promoted to the presidency, who spend their careers enforcing unjust policies. Likewise, there are the victims whose devotion to work may never be acknowledged or rewarded. The church cannot solve basic economic problems. The cause is too deeply rooted. Ultimate solutions must await the return of Christ, who will come to finish what God began in creation. In the meantime the church can assist employees and employers to live with tensions. Providing a forum for people to consider their options or to share frustrations or for factions to learn to talk to one another is one important responsibility.

Facing ambiguities squarely is insufficient as a style of life. There is something appropriate about the conversionist perspective, expressed most clearly today in the views of liberation theologians: The gospel must never become an obstacle to social and political and economic reform. No solution will be ultimate, but some forms of economic organization are more workable and more just than others. God's care for the world should become a stimulus to seek justice, an invitation into a future that is open. If the church cannot prescribe answers, it can at least serve as a stimulus and a forum for discussion.

Employment is an important facet of human life. It is only one facet, however. Much of what the New Testament has to say about work is by way of warning: Work can easily become an end rather than a means, the sole focus of life. It can also become a means to inappropriate ends. Jesus told stories about people whose lives were consumed by possessions, like the rich farmer whose one concern was having sufficient storage capacity for his crops (Luke 12: 13–21). Money and property, like employment, offer an opportunity for service. They also provide great temptation: "How hard it will be for those who have riches to enter the kingdom of God!" Jesus told his followers (Mark 10:23).

Work, furthermore, is not identical with earning a salary. There are many tasks necessary to the operation of our society which require full-time commitment that are unsalaried. Luther's definition of vocation included such tasks as parenting—full-time occupations, requiring energy, patience, and creativity—that result in no income. Our society exerts enormous pressure on a person, however, to earn a salary, nearly equating social worth with salary. The women's movement called attention to the injustices of a society that highly regards employment but systematically excludes women from a whole range of occupational opportunities. In its early phases the movement tended to mirror the values of that society, agreeing on the need to earn an income, demeaning the roles of mother and community volunteer. Recent literature has sought to correct the imbalance.

Our call to walk as children of the light extends to employment. Work will involve us in tension and in moral ambiguity. In our struggle to be faithful in our employment, we recognize that our goals are proximate. Absolute right and wrong may remain hidden. At least part of God's will is clear, however: we work to earn a living for ourselves and our families, and through our work we contribute to the stability and well-being of others. If our employment provides a sense of fulfillment, if it offers the opportunity for heroic deeds, or if it permits us to improve the lot of others and their appreciation of their tasks, we may consider ourselves specially blessed by God.

5

CHRISTIANS AND THE FAMILY

Be subject to one another out of reverence for Christ. Wives, be subject to your husbands, as to the Lord. . . . Husbands, love your wives, as Christ loved the church and gave himself up for her. . . . Children, obey your parents in the Lord, for this is right. (Eph. 5:21 to 6:1)

My grandparents were married in 1915. My grandfather, raised in South Dakota, left the family farm as quickly as he could and headed for the city. He studied dentistry, opened a successful practice in Chicago, and married a preacher's daughter. My grandmother was a musician, a pianist, most of whose life had revolved around the church. After they were married, the young couple had little difficulty sorting out their roles in the home. My grandmother assumed responsibility for running the household and raising the children. She had a few piano students, but most of her time was devoted to her three boys, to making her home a hospitality center for the community, and to a blizzard of activities at the church. My grandfather was responsible for supporting the family. There were hard times, particularly during the depression, but the family managed well. My grandfather spent most of his time at the office, including the mornings he donated to the children's home. He did very little to help out at home. My grandparents lived together for sixty-three years. Though my grandmother wondered occasionally what things would have been like had they been married fifty years later, both she and my grandfather felt fulfilled and satisfied.

The Schmidts live in suburban Philadelphia. Roland is pastor of a small congregation. Elizabeth works in Philadelphia at a part-time job which has grown to thirty hours a week, a job she enjoys very much. They have two children, both in elementary school. Elizabeth commutes to work by train, which means leaving early in the morning before the children have left for school, and returning at suppertime, several hours after school is out. Roland thus assumes responsibility for getting the children off to school and welcoming them home. Since Elizabeth gets only three weeks of vacation, Roland spends a good deal of time with the children in the summer as well, studying at home in the morning, taking them swimming in the afternoon after he has made his calls. The congregation is small enough and sufficiently sympathetic to allow their pastor time for his parental chores. Besides, much of the time he spends at church is in the evening. Elizabeth finds her job stimulating, and it does not seem to interfere with her roles as mother and wife. She spends quality time with her children and with her husband. The couple share domestic responsibilities; Roland particularly enjoys cooking. The arrangement suits the couple, the children, and the church. Roland knows his children better than most fathers, Elizabeth feels fulfilled, and the extra income keeps the family afloat.

Both are examples of Christian families. The two very different patterns are only a sampling of the remarkable diversity that exists within our society. Any consideration of family life among Christians must take into account the variety that exists—and has always existed—within Christendom. There never has been one basic pattern of family

life. Families of believers in other cultures have assigned
roles differently. Children in white families in parts of the
South were customarily raised by a female member of the
household other than the natural mother; often the
woman was black. Wealthy families in the East frequently
sent children off to boarding school at an early age.

In the last decade and a half family life has become even
more complex. Society has undergone a revolution since
my grandparents were married; some would call it dissolu-
tion. Life was simpler in 1915. My grandparents had few
decisions to make about their roles within the home. They
knew what was expected of them and what they could
expect. Today, young couples like the Schmidts must
make many decisions about careers and parental responsibilities. Their children will have even more options. Will
they marry or not? There is less stigma attached to the
single life than fifty years ago, and even if discrimination
exists in the job market, women can support themselves
in a way my grandmother could not. If the children marry,
will they choose to raise a family? Again, more couples are
choosing not to have children, and efficient methods of
contraception make the choice possible. If they decide to
have children, how will responsibilities be shared? Will
both pursue careers? If so, whose career will be primary?
When husband or wife is transferred, how will the family
decide to move or stay?

Young people beginning married life will undoubtedly
find the world a far more interesting place than it was a
half century ago. Women in particular are free to explore
dimensions of their abilities in the world outside the home
and to pursue interests in ways unknown to earlier genera-
tions. The openness has its price, however. Family life is
far more stressful. My students who are graduating from
the seminary—both men and women—must often choose
whether to persuade a spouse to quit his or her job in order
to accept a call to a parish in another town, or to turn down

a call with the hope of finding something nearby. Young wives are more often unwilling to delay their education until their husbands have finished school. Inflexible work schedules make sharing responsibilities for children difficult, causing guilt and resentment. Society has created expectations within families that it is not yet flexible enough to fulfill. The pressures on families are more intense than when my grandparents began their life together.

It is not surprising that there are many people unwilling or unable to live with the uncertainties and stress. Like Archie Bunker, they look back wistfully to a time when "girls were girls and men were men," when people knew what to expect from life and what was expected of them. There seems to be an almost infinite market for books on parenting, on sexual roles, and on the family. The response to the videotaped lectures "Focus on the Family" by Christian psychologist James Dobson has been overwhelming. The whole society seems open for advice on family structure, parenting, and male-female relations.

One response from churches has been a hardening of traditional views. Many Roman Catholic women were deeply troubled by the visit of Pope John Paul II to this country. On the one hand, his personal charisma and his concern for the poor and the oppressed overwhelmed all who met him. On the other hand, his inflexibility regarding the role of women in the church, abortion, and contraception seemed calculated to terminate any discussion about the appropriateness of tradition in contemporary American society. A resurgent conservative Protestant movement has joined the Roman Catholic Church in its opposition to abortion and has spawned production of books and articles spelling out *the* Christian view of parenting, family life, sexuality, and divorce. The attraction of such books is that they give answers. Morality is pictured in legal terms, as obedience to fixed laws, with right and wrong responses to every situation. The liability of such an approach is its inflexibility, its inability to deal with the world as it is. In an ideal world artificial contraception might not be necessary. In countries where population growth is hopelessly out of control and people are starving, it may provide the only practical solution to a desperate problem. Blanket opposition to artificial contraception arises from a view of truth strangely out of touch with the way things are in the world.

A counterresponse among church members in our society has been to disregard Christian tradition in considering how to rear children or to structure family life. As the position of the Roman Catholic Church on contraception has hardened, the number of Catholic women who use contraceptives has increased. Families simply ignore the views of the church. Like the rest of society, they look for advice among experts in the field of medicine or psychology. Fewer women use oral contraceptives, not because the church has declared them morally unacceptable, but because doctors have declared them medically unsafe. Decisions about alternative methods involve sorting out opinions about effectiveness and the impact on sexual performance. Christians look hopefully to pollsters or to psychologists for evidence that premarital sex does or does not enhance married life. That many Christians disregard the views of the church and its tradition does not mean the tradition is wrong or should be shelved. It may mean that greater effort is required relating the tradition to the world as it is—and that a view of morality as involving decisions about absolute right and wrong is as inadequate in the sphere of family life as in politics or business.

Ephesians is a helpful focus for consideration of Christian family life. The passage (5:21 to 6:9) says plainly that women are to submit to their husbands, that children are to obey their parents, and that slaves are to be obedient to their masters. The obvious way to interpret the passage is to assume that the Bible means what it says. One implication would be that households like those of Roland and Elizabeth may well be unchristian, since Elizabeth is by no means submissive. And for precisely that reason, Christians of a liberal cast reject Ephesians as outmoded. They point to the cultural conditionedness of the table of duties in ch. 5. In the first century, slaves were part of the household. We have ceased to believe that slavery is part of a natural order ordained by God; it is now time, the argument goes, to dispense with the notion that wives must be submissive. When women are more capable than men, they should be promoted to positions of authority in the business world. When wives are endowed with more sense and better leadership skills than their husbands, they should serve as head of the family. Paul himself speaks of the end of the law (Rom. 10:4) and of the end of distinctions in baptism ("neither male nor female," Gal. 3:28). And arguments from nature simply do not hold. Though there are biological differences between male and female, the similarities are far more striking. In the human species, sexuality is far more a matter of cultural conditioning than of instinct. Stephen Sapp makes this clear:

> That is, animals are male and female, but hardly "masculine" or "feminine." These latter terms simply do not apply, even when they describe behavior. . . . Thus it appears that "masculine-feminine" is a cultural (and therefore *human*) distinction which is largely determined . . . in the way the child is reared.

Such arguments have considerable weight. Ephesians is a first-century letter. Society was different. Arguments for the exclusive validity of its view of the household from biology, from culture, or from the character of biblical ethics will not be compelling. One important reason is that understanding the ethical advice in Ephesians means locating it in the larger conversation of which it is a part.

When that is done, the advice sounds different. The "table of household duties" in Eph. 5:21 to 6:9 was an ethical commonplace in the first century. Non-Christian moralists employed the table as a useful way of organizing their advice, since they could assume that everyone was a member of a household. In addressing husbands, wives, children, masters, and slaves, they spoke to the whole society, emphasizing basic social responsibilities. The table, with its pattern of relationships, does not pretend to derive family life from the eternal law of God. The duties are expressions of common sense in the Roman world of the first century. Thus the most interesting feature of the whole table of duties may be the opening sentence, advice uncharacteristic of the wider culture: "Be subject to one another out of reverence for Christ" (Eph. 5:21). The statement about mutual subjection is without parallel in the writings of Greek philosophers or Jewish moralists.

The table of duties must also be read in the context of the letter as a whole. Ephesians speaks of faith in extravagant language. Initiates to the new community have been "seated in the heavenly places" (2:6); their corporate life reveals mysteries "to the principalities and powers in the heavenly places" (3:10). The letter seeks to help believers "comprehend with all the saints what is the breadth and length and height and depth" (3:18). The great mysteries to which the author refers, however, turn out to be concrete: that Gentiles are fellow heirs with Jews, that dividing walls of hostility have been broken down, that people can live together in peace. Living as befits those who have been seated in the heavenly places involves ordinary human relationships. Faith does not propel believers into a "spiritual" realm, but into homes. The baptized are called to live as proper husbands, wives, children, masters, and slaves. The ethical advice seems intended to head off tendencies to detach faith from everyday life.

We can appreciate the commonsense wisdom reflected

in Ephesians without regarding the advice as God's unchanging law. The author acknowledges that life in the world requires structure. The family is a microcosm of the state. If our life together requires regulation at the level of communities, the same is true at the level of intimate personal relations. Every human society has recognized the potential of sexuality for good and evil. It offers the possibility of communicating at the most intimate level, and it provides the means of violating intimacy in the most destructive way. The more intense the relationship between people, the greater their vulnerability. When children are born, the potential casualties of a destructive relationship increase.

Every society has thus developed family structures as a way of regulating sexual relations and protecting children. The structures in our own society have become so flexible that they have almost ceased to function as structures. Men and women move in and out of relationships with less regard for the law. Courts have difficulty deciding if parents should be informed of their teenage child's decision to have an abortion. Rigid laws forbidding divorce and supporting absolute authority of parents are unrealistic alternatives in our society. Few would condemn wives or children to a life of domestic abuse from a deranged husband and father. Nevertheless, the possibility for harm to couples, children, and society increases as social agreements about marital commitment and parental responsibility disintegrate. The law will not cure social ills, but it can minimize their destructive potential.

There is another sense in which social structures are necessary. Our lives together depend upon shared roles. Life must be predictable. We need some idea of what others expect of us and what we can expect of them, even if we choose to ignore such expectations. When the life of society loses its shape, each individual is left to define his or her own role. For instance, my children like to know where the boundaries are, and they frequently experiment to see how far they can push my wife and me. They may not agree with our values or rules, but the boundaries allow them to establish their own. The prospect of having nothing by which to gauge what is appropriate behavior between men and women, no male or female roles against which to test individual behavior, no guidelines by which to measure good parenting—that prospect is chilling. There is little justification for reading the table of duties in Ephesians as an expression of the eternal, unchangeable law of God. There is every reason to respect the need for structure within family life even among Christians who have been set free from bondage to the law.

Family life in our society reflects deep-seated social values. If life is lived on a spectrum between novelty and regularity, we have chosen to err on the side of novelty. Individual freedom is a primary virtue. We have made every effort to cultivate creativity and individual expression. The extraordinary variety in family patterns mirrors our view of life. The same is true in other cultures that have quite different values. The Chinese have valued regularity above novelty, and their family life embodies a distinctive philosophy. I recall seeing a mother in our town pushing her twins down the street in a stroller built for two. Both children faced the front, seated side by side, with a tray for toys in front of each. In a stroller that a Chinese mother was using for her twins, the two infants sat facing each other, with a common tray for toys between. From the very beginning, children in that culture learn they must live together. Individuality is less important than cooperation. We may still prefer our own way of life, but we should be realistic about its liabilities. The clamor for guidelines for family structure among Christians reflects good sense. The table of duties in Ephesians can provide a basis for conversation without having to be read as an inflexible regulation.

The movement in Ephesians from salvation to human relations likewise offers a helpful direction for reflection. Christ's self-giving love serves as a model of society at its most basic level. Love that arises from commitment promises the deepest and most fulfilling relationships. I can dare to open myself to my wife, to become vulnerable, because we have made promises to each other that we can trust. We have agreed to grow together and to grow old together. In another sense, Christ's love is not only an example for husband and wife but is something that makes the relationship possible. It is God's commitment to us and the promise of an unfailing love that let us dare to look into ourselves and to open ourselves to one another. For Christians, family life is more conformity to Christ than imitation of him. It is more a gift of grace than an achievement.

DIVORCE

In a small suburban congregation of forty families, a pastor whom I know counseled with five couples in a single year whose marriages ended in divorce. The couples were pillars of the congregation. In not one case was infidelity the reason for divorce. No one really understood what had happened. The couples simply decided they no longer loved one another and could not live together. In other cases, infidelity is a factor. More than one graduate student I know who was supported through school by his wife found a new mate as soon as school was finished. At my fifteenth college class reunion I soon quit asking classmates about families and spouses. The number of divorces was extraordinary. If the statistics have lost their ability to shock, involvement in a friend's painful separation serves as a reminder that behind the statistics lie human tragedies.

No one knows exactly why so many marriages break down in our culture, though most people are agreed that the reasons lie deep within our social systems. One reason is certainly that women can support themselves financially and no longer need to remain in a destructive relationship. Others point to a general decline in personal commitment and responsibility in a permissive society. Still others fault courting patterns and an extended developmental pattern that keeps young people in school, where they have few adult decisions to make, until their twenties—by which time many have selected mates. Still more radical analysts argue that the traditional marriage was necessary when women could not support themselves and was viable when people rarely lived beyond their forties. The problem, they insist, is that the old structure no longer fits a society where people live into their seventies and where women no longer need the protection and support of males.

Christians must participate in such analysis, since there will not be a cure for domestic tragedies unless we understand the causes. In the meantime, the church must help people learn how to deal with brokenness. Seward Hiltner once commented that Christians seem willing to apply justification and forgiveness to every aspect of human life but marriage. One reason is perhaps that hurts inflicted within the families can be the most painful. Divorces affect children as well as adults. Nevertheless, brokenness is a condition of human life in a fallen world. There is little justification for withholding the healing power of the gospel from those who have sinned and fallen short in their relations with spouses. Jesus forbade divorce, but he also prevented the execution of a woman caught in adultery and he gave his life "as a ransom for many" (Mark 10:45). "Those who are well have no need of a physician," he told those who objected to the company he kept, "but those who are sick" (Mark 2:17).

Ministering to the victims of broken homes does not mean apologizing for the Christian tradition's high regard for marriage and marital fidelity. Grace is not the same as indifference. Society as well as the church has an investment in ordered relationships between men and women. Marital vows provide couples with the protection of the law and testify to the character of love as commitment. The Bible will continue to view divorce as a transgression of God's will as well as of the natural order. But Christians will continue to live in a world that is in bondage to sin and death, a world in which "natural" is seldom the rule. In that imperfect world, even the structures of marriage will not guarantee wholeness, and the casualties of broken homes will require healing. A greater investment in premarital counseling and in marriage enrichment programs is an important, if partial, response from churches. Analysis of cultural patterns by experts inside and outside the church will continue. Until there are fundamental changes in our society, however, Christians will continue to live with brokenness, suspended in the tension between justice and mercy, law and gospel.

THE SINGLE LIFE

I got a taste of what it is like to be a single adult when I attended a pastors' conference last year without my wife. The annual conference, held at a fine resort, was an occasion for couples to gather for recreation and relaxation as well as for a few lectures. Pastors and spouses look forward to the conference as a chance to see old friends.

I attended the event as a new member of the synod. I knew almost no one. I soon came to dread mealtime. Food was served buffet style. Standing in line was not too uncomfortable, because there was usually time for introductions and a friendly chat. By the time I had filled my plate with food, however, my new acquaintances had vanished into the dining room. The tables in the dimly lighted room were all set for eight. At every meal, I ended up sitting with three couples I had never met who were engaged in lively conversation when I arrived at the table. It was quite clear that I did not fit.

I can understand a bit more clearly what a woman told me who had been widowed six months earlier. "I never realized," she said, "how much of my life was tied to my husband's. We did everything as a couple—played bridge, attended dinner parties. Now that I am alone, I rarely go out. After all, who invites singles to an evening of bridge? What couple invites a single to a dinner party? No one buys five or seven or nine place settings of china—you always buy six or eight or ten. The world is for couples, not singles."

Coming from a widow of only six months, the words are perhaps a bit exaggerated. Nevertheless, her assessment is partly true. Our culture, and the church in particular, views marriage as the natural state. It used to be a rule in the Lutheran church that congregations would not call an unmarried pastor. Since the seminary forbade marriage during the years of schooling, there was a scramble after graduation to find a mate. Though the church is more flexible today, single pastors are still the center of attention for well-intentioned matchmakers. Marriage seems more natural. The "singles" group in most congregations, if there is such a group, is often set apart from other adult organizations. One congregation tried to include them in a joint program, calling the group "Pairs and Spares." The humor could not mask the implied values of the congregation.

It is even misleading to speak of "singles" as though together they were a uniform group. Some have never married, others have been divorced, still others have lost a spouse through death. Some are single parents, others have no children. The needs of singles are thus different. Single parents may have more in common with couples in the congregation than with the unmarried. Isolation of singles may guarantee that some will never have important needs met.

One thing Christians can do is to understand the validity of the single life and extend the same support to the unmarried as to the married. The Roman Catholic tradition valued celibate life more highly than married life. Protestants may have overcompensated. The apostle Paul was far more relaxed about the whole matter. He discusses the question under the heading of "gifts" (I Cor. 7:7). Christians are free to marry or not, depending on their "gift." For reasons of his own, Paul preferred the single life. Advising against marriage had nothing to do with a low view of human sexuality or with a belief that the single life was a "higher" calling. He simply felt that in view of the little time the world had left (in his opinion), it was better not to undertake long-range projects like marriage (I Cor. 7: 25–31). The Corinthians expected a definite answer to the question about whether it was better to be married or unmarried. Paul refused to offer more than his personal opinion.

Those baptized into Christ are free to respond to God's call. The single life may be an exception in society, but it is not therefore better or worse than being married. It is simply different. One of the marks of a community of the redeemed is its ability to accept diversity without having to evaluate. People who have lived without spouses have made enormous contributions to society and to the church and have lived full lives. Their vocation is neither higher nor lower than that of men and women who live their lives together. It is simply different.

Precisely for such people, however, the church can provide a place where they can feel at home. The Gospels even speak of the community of believers as a family:

Jesus said, "Truly, I say to you, there is no one who has left house or brothers or sisters or mother or father or children

or lands, for my sake and for the gospel, who will not receive
a hundredfold now in this time, houses and brothers and
sisters and mothers and children and lands, with persecu-
tions, and in the age to come eternal life." (Mark 10:29–30)

All of us need intimacy. We need friends to laugh and
cry with, people who will listen to us and talk to us, people
in whose eyes we can catch some glimpse of who we are.
Such intimacy is possible within the family. Many for
whom Mark wrote, however, had been excluded from
their homes and communities because of their faith in
Christ. For such displaced persons, the church provided a
new family. Though the reasons are different, many in our
society are without a family. The community of believers
is called to support families, but it can also serve as a family
for those who have none. It can be a place where friend-
ships are born, where life can be nurtured, differences
tolerated, wounds healed, joys and sorrows shared. Perhaps that is what Ephesians means when it refers to the
faithful as "members of the household of God" (Eph. 2:19).

6

THE PEACE OF GOD
AND LIFE BETWEEN THE TIMES

We have examined discipleship by focusing on various spheres within which the life of faith is lived out. Followers of Christ are called first into the fellowship of the church, the new community in Christ that is to embody the liberating and reconciling power of the gospel. Christians are not called out of the world, however. Walking worthy of the gospel leads into the everyday, involving our roles as citizens, as employees and employers, and as family members. Life cannot be separated into compartments. Paul's definition of proper worship as "presenting your bodies as a living sacrifice, holy and acceptable to God" (Rom. 12:1) prevents confining religion to the church. As "bodies," we are necessarily children of the world, tied into a network of relationships that make up society. We depend upon others for food and clothing and are thus economically interdependent; we rely on others for protection under the law and are thus politically related; we depend upon families for nurture and support. God enlists "bodies" in his service; discipleship involves all of life.

It is the social dimensions of human life that make discipleship complex. American Protestantism has tended to focus on private religious experience. We speak of sin as individual transgression of God's law, of justification as

forgiveness of those sins; sanctification involves "pommel-
ing our bodies and subduing them." Evil manifests itself
not only as individual transgression, however, but as a
power that perverts our corporate life. We harm people
even when we intend to do good. In the political and
economic arena, we deal with partial solutions and genuine moral ambiguities. Our personal rules may not apply.
Service to God and neighbor in the world involves living
with God's silence. Utility is not the final test of truth, but
however moral a particular economic proposal may sound,
if it does not work, the poor will not be fed and neither will
the rich. Discipleship in the world thus demands a willingness to experiment. Paul says that we must "prove [i.e.,
test by experience] what is the will of God, what is good
and acceptable and perfect" (Rom. 12:2). We should be
ready to learn from experience and from others, to disagree and to change our minds. Certainty will be possible
only when we no longer see through a glass dimly, but
face-to-face.

Progress and growth are thus not the primary categories
by which biblical authors speak about individual discipleship. Paul can speak about being "transformed by the
renewal of your mind"; his letters are full of genuine ex-
hortations. But he also acknowledges our participation in
a creation that "groans in travail," awaiting the birth of a
new age. Jesus assured his followers that until his return,
they could expect opposition and conflict. Ephesians
speaks of battles yet to be fought. The final defeat of death,
though certain, lies still in the future. Until then, Christians live in anticipation. The life of faith is life between
the times.

Ephesians seeks to locate believers in time and space. It
plants the church firmly in the world and in the present.
It speaks of anticipation, but more often of remembering.
Understanding discipleship means recalling what God has
done—both for the world and for the recipients of the

letter. The goal of all the "knowing" (knowing "what is the hope to which he has called you," Eph. 1:18; knowing "what is the immeasurable greatness of his power in us who believe," 1:19; comprehending "with all the saints what is the breadth and length and height and depth," 3:18) is peace—not peace as the absence of conflict or as the surrender of hope, but peace as a sense of wholeness, arising from confidence that things make sense, that beyond the tensions and ambiguities is a God who has ultimate control of life.

The need for peace of that sort is embedded deep in our being. In our society the need is largely unmet. There was a time when our authors and artists believed that order was the greatest threat to our society. The development of technology seemed to offer leaders an almost limitless potential for controlling the shape of public and private life. Aldous Huxley in his *Brave New World* and George Orwell in his *1984* held up for all to see the dreaded specter of a world without choices, a world of enforced sameness. Their writings issued an eloquent call to battle for individual rights and opportunities for creative self-expression.

As 1984 approaches, advances in technology have not resulted in enforced order. They seem, rather, to have contributed to greater disorder. We are bombarded with more information than we can possibly process. There is scarcely a pain we do not share through the medium of the evening news. Heroes are systematically dismembered before an audience of millions. Politics has become public, and the complexities of governing the society are so overwhelming that presidents will probably last no more than a single term. The family, the focal point and proving ground of all societies, has been subjected to devastating centrifugal forces. It is possible that we are living in a time of transition, as Alvin Toffler suggests in his book *The Third Wave*, when inadequate social structures are being replaced by new forms, but thus far no new comprehensive structure has emerged. We are being pulled apart into smaller and smaller enclaves, with fewer and fewer shared traditions. The situation comedies that comprise the bulk of evening television aptly mirror a society that is a bizarre collection of individuals in every conceivable situation all trying to feel good about themselves. Artists and musicians no longer provide for society a vision of beauty and harmony; they mirror a world of confused, solitary beings. "The reason I like baroque music," a friend said, "is that it was composed by musicians who believed in God and who thought life made sense. We aren't so sure about the first and we've absolutely given up on the second."

If the realities to which the gospel had to speak during the time of the Reformation were a shared sense of guilt and terror at the prospect of eternal punishment, in our time the gospel must address a shared sense of fragmentation and incoherence. In this respect, our experience of life is remarkably similar to that of Christians in the first century. Their world had fallen apart. Communities that had been swallowed up by the Roman Empire lost their sense of local tradition and were deluged with new customs and information. Life seemed out of their control. Families were torn apart. The people needed to know that life held together, that the world made sense, that behind "the dim unknown" God waited in the shadows, "keeping watch above his own." They needed peace.

Sermons as we can see them in the New Testament were not weekly calls to repentance. They sought, rather, to help congregations understand how life made sense, how God was present in their lives, what it meant in their present circumstances to be people for whom Christ had died as they awaited his final return. Baptism served as a constant reminder that God had claimed them in a way that did not have to be repeated. In the Lord's Supper, they celebrated God's continued presence among them.

In telling stories about Jesus and about other Christians, they sought to gain some sense of the shape of life. The rhythm of that corporate life provided them with a "shield against terror," the image Peter Berger uses to describe the purpose of religion.

Our religious heritage can provide structure for our lives which is lacking in our culture. The ritual of the church, the discipline of private devotion, and regular reading of the Scriptures are not ends in themselves. They serve to remind us of what God has done for us in the past and also of his continuing presence. Christian rites encompass life from birth to grave. Baptism or dedication of children as a corporate event testifies to God's acceptance of us even prior to our deserving and enlists the resources of the Christian family in the nurture of children. Various rites of passage, whether first communion or confirmation, recognize the need for new expressions of the faith and acknowledge God's love for adolescents as well as children and adults. Marriage rites as public congregational functions announce God's blessings on families and acknowledge the need families have for the support of others. Funeral rites offer an opportunity to share the grief of those near us while also recognizing that we are in God's hands even in death. Regular celebration of the Lord's Supper provides consistent testimony to the availability of God's forgiveness and sustenance. At every stage of life, at every moment, God is present, keeping watch over his children.

Life has drama. There are risks, possibilities for growth, opportunities for victories as well as defeats until the day God finishes what he began. The life of faith also has a rhythm, an order and a structure that offers peace amid chaos. "Peace I leave with you," said Jesus, "my peace I give to you; not as the world gives do I give it to you" (John 14:27). Whether we succeed or fail in altering the course of our lives or the course of history, whether we achieve prominence or live our lives in the shadows, whether we have the opportunity to perform a heroic deed or not, we can find sustenance in the gospel which has called us from darkness to light. The life of faith begins with God's gift of love, and it is sustained by the promise that his love will not fail us:

> Now to him who by the power at work within us is able to do far more abundantly than all that we ask or think, to him be glory in the church and in Christ Jesus to all generations, for ever and ever. Amen. (Eph 3:20–21)

)

QUESTIONS FOR DISCUSSION

Chapter 1. THE CHURCH'S BOOK

1. How do you think the Scripture lessons for the Sunday service (or other services of worship) should be selected?

2. When you want help or advice from the Bible, how do you determine where to look and what is relevant?

3. To what extent does it matter to you whether a particular belief or practice is "biblical" or not? What constitutes a "biblical" statement or action?

4. What biblical texts or broader biblical understandings would you find applicable to each of the issues of current public debate discussed in the section "The Bible in Theology"?

Chapter 2. CRISIS AND CANON

1. How effective are the programs and practices of Bible reading and Bible study in your church?

2. How would you characterize your own approach to the Bible in relation to those described in this chapter?

3. What were the earliest Christian Scriptures? In what sense were they "Christian"?

4. How did the New Testament come into being and

as the women's movement or ERA? On what grounds would you argue for a particular point of view?

Chapter 2. CHRISTIANS AND THE WORLD

1. In what sense do you find the plurality of views about life in the world within the New Testament liberating? In what sense is the plurality threatening?

2. How would you contrast a "Christian" view of the world in the United States, El Salvador, Poland, South Africa, or the Soviet Union? Do you find Niebuhr's categories helpful in thinking about such questions?

3. Where do you think your own tradition fits within Niebuhr's categories or within the biblical tradition?

4. Spend some time discussing Bolt's *A Man for All Seasons.* To what extent is More's conservative approach justified by the biblical tradition or by common sense?

5. How appropriate are the criticisms of liberation theologians for your church, whether on the local or the national level? To what extent does your church hinder attempts to secure justice for all? How actively does the church seek to expose laws that discriminate against the poor and the powerless?

Chapter 3. CHRISTIANS AND THE STATE

1. What is the historical stance of your church regarding the relationship of the church to the state? How appropriate do you believe that position is in our present setting?

2. Conservative Christianity in this country has traditionally reflected a Baptist view of the separation of church and state. To what do you attribute the new political activism among conservative Christians—i.e., coalitions of Christian groups supporting particular candidates or issues in the name of the gospel? What are the possibilities of such changes, both positive and negative?

3. From William Stringfellow to Billy Graham, Christian leaders from both ends of the political and religious spectrum have begun to speak with passion about the danger of the arms race. In what ways should Christians and churches take up the issue of peace? What would be an appropriate form of involvement within your particular tradition?

4. As churches contemplate involvement in the affairs of the state, what differences might there be in the shape of that involvement in a pluralistic society like ours from the involvement of a state church in England or Scandinavia or Germany?

5. Locate a policy statement from your national church offices about a particular affair of state and discuss its appropriateness in the light of the biblical material discussed in this chapter or in the light of Niebuhr's categories.

Chapter 4. VOCATION AND OCCUPATION

1. What actual messages does the church—your congregation and the national body—communicate about the task of the laity in the world? To what extent is there a difference between the actual message and the official views of the church?

2. How frequently within the life of your congregation are there occasions for discussing the difficulties of relating Christian faith to vocation and occupation? How might such opportunities be increased?

3. To what degree do you find it helpful to think of your work in terms of its positive function as a way of serving family and neighbor? To what extent is it necessary and helpful to think of work as a necessary response to the reality of evil in the world?

4. In our culture where work is so central to our sense of personal worth, what are we to do when there are not enough jobs for everyone? What is Christian vocation in a

community where there is chronic unemployment?

5. How can we properly recognize and reward un-salaried work that is beneficial to society? In what ways can the growing number of retired people provide models for service to society and church that reflects a proper sense of vocation but that is not rewarded financially? How could we separate work from salary?

6. Discuss some of the ways in which workers and professionals might find assistance either within your congregation or outside in their concern about their occupational roles in the light of the Christian tradition.

Chapter 5. CHRISTIANS AND THE FAMILY

1. In what ways has the women's movement significantly changed the way people in your community view family life? How could those changes provide an agenda for the church's ministry to families?

2. What is a typical family in your community? What are the major factors that determine the day-to-day shape of family activity (school, athletic programs, commuting patterns, etc.)? How is the church's ministry to families related to those various factors?

3. In what sense does the program of your congregation serve to reinforce family ties and to what extent is it just another occasion for separating spouses, children, and grandparents? How might the program better serve families?

4. What provisions are made within the congregation for single parents, for couples without children, or for singles? What message does your church communicate about the single life?

5. How can the church both heal the victims of broken homes and continue to support the family as a viable institution in our society?

6. What bearing do recent changes in the legal defini-

tion of contractual relationships between two people (i.e., the Lee Marvin case) have on the church's attitude toward marriage? How can we separate religious and legal issues? What stake does the church as church have in the institution of marriage?

Chapter 6. THE PEACE OF GOD AND LIFE BETWEEN THE TIMES

1. A sense of identity is often communicated through shared stories. What were the stories that gave you a sense of what it meant to be a Christian and an American when you were young? What stories, if any, give our children their identity?

2. How does the gospel as it is preached and taught in your congregation offer a way of understanding life in a comprehensive manner? What areas of life are apt to be excluded from consideration?

3. To what extent does the life of the congregation provide a rhythm for its members? How important are baptisms for the community? To what extent are church weddings expected? Are funerals held at the church or at a funeral home? Why?

4. What are the major factors that determine the rhythm of our lives and offer some sense of what life is about? What does the church's tradition have to do with such factors?

REFERENCES

In this volume reference is made to the following books and periodicals, which are listed in the order of their use.

Chapter 1. THE NEW COMMUNITY IN CHRIST

Joseph Hertz, *Authorized Daily Prayer Book,* rev. ed. (Bloch Publishing Co., 1948), pp. 19–21.

Chapter 2. CHRISTIANS AND THE WORLD

H. Richard Niebuhr, *Christ and Culture* (Harper & Row, 1951).

Robert Bolt, *A Man for All Seasons* (Random House, 1960), pp. 65–67.

Daniel Migliore, *Called to Freedom* (Westminster Press, 1980), pp. 15, 14.

Jürgen Moltmann, *The Crucified God,* tr. by R. A. Wilson and John Bowden (Harper & Row, 1974), pp. 329–335.

Chapter 3. CHRISTIANS AND THE STATE

William Golding, *Lord of the Flies* (Coward, McCann & Geoghegan, 1978), pp. 186–187.

Hal Lindsey, *The Late Great Planet Earth* (Zondervan

115

Publishing House, 1970), p. 94.

William Stringfellow, *Conscience and Obedience* (Word Books, 1977), p. 111.

James E. Wallis, "Solidarity," *Sojourners,* Vol. 11, Jan. 1982, p. 4.

Martin Luther, "Against the Robbing and Murdering Hordes of Peasants," in *The Christian in Society,* ed. by Robert Schulz, Vol. 46 of *Luther's Works* (Fortress Press, 1967), pp. 45–56.

Reinhold Niebuhr, *The Nature and Destiny of Man* (Charles Scribner's Sons, 1941), Vol. 1, p. 298.

Jürgen Moltmann, *The Theology of Hope,* tr. by J. Leitsch (Harper & Row, 1967), p. 312.

Chapter 4. VOCATION AND OCCUPATION

Ronald F. Hock, *The Social Context of Paul's Ministry: Tentmaking and Apostleship* (Fortress Press, 1980), p. 37.

William E. Diehl, *Christianity and Real Life* (Fortress Press, 1976), pp. 73–78.

Martin Luther, quoted in Gustaf Wingren, *Luther on Vocation,* tr. by Carl C. Rasmussen (Muhlenberg Press, 1957), p. 72.

Martin Luther, quoted in George Forell, *Faith Active in Love* (Augsburg Publishing House, 1954), pp. 150–151.

Chapter 5. CHRISTIANS AND THE FAMILY

Stephen Sapp, *Sexuality, the Bible, and Science* (Fortress Press, 1977), p. 92.

Chapter 6. THE PEACE OF GOD AND LIFE BETWEEN THE TIMES

Peter Berger, *The Sacred Canopy* (Doubleday & Co., 1967).

FOR FURTHER READING

Becker, Ernest. *The Denial of Death.* Free Press, 1973.
Birch, Bruce, and Rasmussen, Larry. *Bible and Ethics in the Christian Life.* Augsburg Publishing House, 1976.
Bonhoeffer, Dietrich. *Life Together,* tr. and with an Introduction by John W. Doberstein. Harper & Row, 1954.
Keck, Leander. *The New Testament Experience of Faith.* Bethany Press, 1977.

Fine collections of information about the place of women in Greco-Roman society are found in Wayne Meeks, "The Image of the Androgene," *History of Religions,* Vol. 13 (1974), pp. 165–208, and Joachim Jeremias, *Jerusalem in the Time of Jesus,* tr. by F. H. and C. H. Cave (Fortress Press, 1969).
A brief discussion of the contemporary debate over Paul's view of women, with a helpful bibliography, can be found in Calvin J. Roetzel, *The Letters of Paul* (John Knox Press, 1975), pp. 99–102.